PASSING OBAMACARE

by

Glenn Troy Morton

Copyright © Glenn Troy Morton, 2011
All rights reserved.

Without limiting the rights under copyright reserved above, no part of this publication may be reproduced, stored in or introduced into a retrieval system, or transmitted, in any form, or by any means (electronic, mechanical, photocopying, recording, or otherwise), without the prior written permission of the copyright owner.

The scanning, uploading, and distribution of this book via the internet or via any other means without the permission of the copyright owner is illegal and punishable by law. Please purchase only authorized electronic editions, and do not participate in or encourage electronic piracy of copyrighted materials. Your support of the author's rights is appreciated.

This book is dedicated to my wife Alicia, who had the love and courage to marry me, and to my daughter Taylor, who motivated me to follow my heart. You both make me the happiest man on the face of the earth!

Acknowledgements

Thank you God for choosing me to send this message. I love you...

Thanks to my mom (Iris Morton), my Grandma (Iris Fagans), my brother (Davaughn Paige), my wife (Alicia Morton), my children (Taylor and Levi Morton), and my step-children (Abby and Jakobi Bradford) for the love and support. I love you!

My deepest thanks to the people in my present, and my past, who shared their knowledge with me over the years. You contributed greatly to the creation of this publication, and I appreciate our lively debates on the issues of the day.

Many thanks to the wonderful and intelligent co-workers who have suffered through my diatribes over the years: Mark Reid, Howard Rankin, John Gardiner, Dan Donoghue, William Bacon, Joseph Finzel, Jessie Gittens, Halbert Carmichael, Nader Barakat, Lennie Moore, Dawn Page, Dorothy Jackson, Colin Romine, Robert Beja, Ann McDermott, and Christina Zettner.

Special thanks to the numerous "best friends" I've had in my life: Mark Dennis, Kevin Chichester, Malcolm Stewart, Meryl Williams, Afriye Amerson, Michelle Smith, Marla

Weaver, Patrick Barnett, Randy Gray, Cedric Harrison, Terrance Hill (who told me to stay true to myself...love you, man!), Jerry Harper, Alodie Maytas, Khalipha Tijani, and Crystal Hines (who told me once that *I* was enough...love you!).

Extra special thanks to those whose acts of selflessness and kindness inspire people like me to reach beyond the boundaries of our lives and make the world a better place. Whether Democrat, Republican, Tea Party, or Independent, your contributions to the greatest country in the world are truly remarkable!

Super Extra Special thanks to Victor Dorobantu at MyCaricature.com. He's versatile, inventive, and a phenomenal artist...much more than a typical caricaturist. It has been a real pleasure watching the image in my head come to life by his hand...

Table of Contents

Prologue — viii

Preface — xxii

Introduction — xxviii

Chapter One
Wake Up Call — 1

Chapter Two
Better to have bad luck than no luck at all? — 9

Chapter Three
Out of Many, One — 16

Chapter Four
One of these things is not like the other — 24

Chapter Five
Obamacare…Do you want this? — 32

Chapter Six
A solution that isn't this, doesn't do that, and won't offend anyone's morality — 39

Chapter Seven
Foundation of Change — 50

Final Chapter
The Way it is — 71

Author's Biography — 83

Notes — 85

Prologue

An Open Letter to President Obama

Hey President Obama,
What's up! How the heck are you? It's been awhile since we've gotten together. I imagine you've been busy, though, so I'm cool!

Listen, I'm sorry to reach out to you in this way, but your BlackBerry's going straight to voice mail, and I'm pretty sure I'm not in your "5", so I didn't know what else to do. I'm starting to think you're forgetting me, what with new friends and a new job taking up your time.

I remember you.

You were my best friend once, weren't you? We used to have so much in common. We were both outsiders; never quite fittin' in no matter how hard we tried (and we tried awfully hard...LOL!).

Do you remember letting Nancy lock you in a hall locker in 7th grade because she said she'd kiss you?! I can't *believe* you fit into such a small space with ears that big! How did you breathe? I understand why you squeezed in, though…she was FINE!

I also recall Harry convincing you to smoke weed for the first time. I <u>told</u> you he was a pothead! I've always wanted to ask if getting high was worth the beating you took when you got home. Even today, I get ghost pains, and I just *heard* what happened :o)

Man, we hung together constantly! We never could score with the ladies (except the one time with Sarah and Michelle B…that was WILD! I <u>still</u> have paw prints…), but were probably the only 2 guys in Punahou High who could, on Monday mornings, cite chapter and verse of the previous Sundays McLaughlin group…

Like you used to say: "Bro's before Ho's!"

Remember when we read the Encyclopedia Britannica after school? Your grandma would make us those ham and pineapple sandwiches with a tall glass of papaya juice. She loved us kids so much, I wanted her to be MY grandma. I miss her!

Hey…did you know I dreamt *we* would be in the encyclopedia for something one day? I'd be president and you'd be MVP of the NBA! Crazy dreams, huh? You couldn't dunk and I'm black…no way we had a chance!

Well, at least not until you. Now, I'm practicing my jump shot and takin' my talents to South Beach!

I mean…you won, B-Easy! You actually WON!

Passing Obamacare

Who cares if no encyclopedias are being printed? If they were on the shelf, a whole chapter would be dedicated to you!

I didn't get a chance to tell you this when everything was going down...too busy celebrating, I guess.

But...B-Regal, I've never been so proud of someone in my whole life!

President Barack Hussein Obama, indeed!

To witness you taking the stage, becoming President of the ENTIRE FREAKIN WORLD! Who would've thunk it? You always wanted to be the best at everything, but you <u>certainly</u> outdid yourself this time. It says a lot about you that you could convince the whole country to even consider electing a not-only-white president.

It was so *hard* being biracial in our younger days. The teasing, getting bullied, and never hanging with the coolest guys in school...

America is a strange, wonderful place, huh?

Hey B-Dazzle, this may be a little off topic, but I wished you had my back when Bully McCain punched me in the face for kissing Olympia. I should've just fought him myself, but I didn't possess the heart to beat him. He's so mean, and I'm not. I might've had more balls if I knew you would fight with me. I thought you'd do anything to help me, being my best buddy and all.

But...water under the bridge, right?

Glenn Troy Morton

Now you're President, and everybody's lining up to be your friend…even the ones in Indonesia who threw rocks at you and made you eat lunch off the floor in Cub Scouts! They never spoke your name while you were in the state senate, did they? I guess saying kind things is easier if you've got your hand out. How much foreign aid do we give them, anyway? You should make them donate a hefty contribution to the presidential library, or build an Obama statue smack in downtown Jakarta!

And the Hawaiians! OH MY GOSH! So funny you're a "native" son now, when the Mokes treated you worse than Haole on Kill Haole Day. I didn't think bandwagons were waterproof!

You and I, though…we are real friends!

Remember going to the b-ball court after class and schooling 'em? You handled the rock, and I manned the paint! Even if Haley, Joe, Eric, and John wouldn't let us play, we just played after they left and still had fun, right? No need to take a beating and come back for more in those days!

Plus, at least we had Bobby J. to pick on…

Seems like so long ago! I should've known you'd follow your dreams to the big stage! Extremely proud of the political career, dude…brings back many good memories *when I watch you and Michelle dancing repeatedly on YouTube.* Such a tear-jerker!

You always said getting to class a few hours before everyone else would pay off. I'm happy things worked out for you, and even happier to be able to call you a friend. I miss the moments we spent together.

They were good times, huh?

What are days like for you now, B-Riddle? I'm worried about you whenever I see you on television. You look different. Heavier, if you know what I mean...

I started noticing the change right after you got elected. Having so many humans put their hopes and dreams on your back is pretty heady stuff. I don't suspect a person in the history of the world has had the amount of people wishing stuff on them as you have had wished on you. Even Jesus Himself didn't inspire followers from Egypt to Philadelphia, only to hear Fox news talking crap about Him afterwards. I genuinely felt for you, carrying so much pressure on your shoulders...

...until I realized you asked for the burden.

Hope and Change, remember? How 'bout "We are the change we have been seeking"? "Fired up! Ready to go!" perhaps???

Hmmmm...

You promised a ton, B-Diddly! You could've guaranteed good governance, a return to prosperity, or something human beings can actually *measure*, and left well enough alone.

Instead, you pledged **transformation**. Did you plan to deliver on a promise so huge?

Glenn Troy Morton

Maybe you had no choice. The election of the first black President, in a country with our history, is transformational in and of itself.

However, from my vantage point, it seemed like you *wanted* Gandhi/Martin Luther King-type love, and you got it. You enjoyed wowing us with your mastery of words, didn't you? It must feel pretty powerful to hear millions chanting "O-Bama!" whenever you have something to say. Hell, if my wife ever chanted my name because I speechified (or chanted my name, period :o), I would be so full of myself, my head would explode!

You had **Germany** at hello!

Oh, and are you kidding me? The Nobel freakin' Peace Prize!? You haven't even peed on the Presidential toilet seat yet!

I guess it's dawning on you by now that wanting is one thing; *promising* is quite another. Promises must be kept, or else you're a liar. Could the reason for the heaviness I noticed in your eyes be the difference between speaking as an inspirational figure and governing as a President? As important as he was, Martin Luther King never ran a country; he only talked about it...

B-Diesel, please don't take this the wrong way, but stubbornness isn't one of your stronger personality traits. You talk a good game, yet are too considerate at times to stand strong against the opinions of others. You're like the point guard who runs an offense well, and is blessed with knowledge and nuance few can claim, but looks for the open man to make the winning shot. Great attribute for a team player; not as useful a trait in a President.

As President, you gotta be Kobe or Mike, not LeBron. Your determination must be to win, not to be a key part of a winning team.

There is a difference, and the difference is heart...

As Achilles said in Troy: "I want what all men want. I just want it more."

When you cause people to *believe* you can provide the power to positively change our country by voting for you, you should own not only the cahones to say it; you need the steel to get it done.

You must possess the will to win, even if you have to be an asshole to get there.

Do you recall your predecessor? The one everyone hated because he was completely and unapologetically wrong about so many things? Remarkably lacking in intellect...the "C" student who invaded Iraq on the vague notion that Arabs and Persians would see democratic freedom and want some for themselves? Remember the millions of people around the world who cursed his name, burned him in effigy, and made him out to be the anti-Christ? How about the footage of Saddam wiping his feet on a rug with the President's face on the top, or the "intellectual elite" who thought he was so stupid because he couldn't enunciate his words correctly?

What was his name again?

Oh yeah…that Bush guy! He was a major league ASSHOLE!

And he was freakin' RIGHT!

I don't want to give him one ounce of credit, but I can't avoid the YouTube clips of him talking about spreading democracy in the middle east and people rising up to overthrow their dictators. I keep contorting my mouth to say "Well, even a broken clock is right twice a day ", yet can't turn on AL Jazeera without feeling like a jackass.

Arabs eyeballed images of purple fingers and free Iraqi's and wanted some of the free vote thang for themselves, and are now toppling governments all over the Middle East like dominoes!

Rather than blame us for their problems, they were offended, and inspired, by our bold action to change their circumstances. We put our blood and treasure on the line for their freedom, and now they are too. And, true to our word, we didn't take one dime from Iraq. We've actually given quite a lot of money to Iraq, and all the expertise we had to offer. Iraq is now free because of us, and not Al Qaeda.

So is Egypt, which is where Al Qaeda was born and raised, and 9-11 actually began. How many of them do you think are planning to attack America now?

The threat level has to be pretty damn low, unless you're Anderson Cooper.

Passing Obamacare

What size balls did the man possess to catch such considerable crap from everyone and still do what he thought was right? How much security must live in his soul to enable him to take on all comers and stick to his guns?

He had a freakin' SHOE thrown at his face, for Christ's sake! TWICE!!

Even I hated his guts, and now I'm enjoying a little hot sauce on my crow, thank you very much; it taste better fried, by the way…

The reason you took a shellacking in the 2010 mid-term elections is your apparent unwillingness to stand up for us. Didn't you know we'd back you up?

America loves you.

I'm not saying you aren't accomplishing a lot; you are, though the accomplishments so far are easier to pass when a President is working with the largest legislative majority in Congress since the Great Depression and no members of the opposing party who want a say.

I'm saying you're not accomplishing enough, because you promised *transformation*, and you haven't taken a shot to win the game.

The game isn't pay equality, gay rights, consumer protections, or saving Wall Street. In basketball parlance, those actions, and the dozens of similar ones, are terrific assists.

Glenn Troy Morton

The game is one class of people taking wealth from the other, even if they have to bankrupt the entire country in the process.

The winning shot would be punishing those who are stealing money from us; who are taking away our homes, our jobs, and our worth. People who are partying with our retirements and foreclosing on our children's' futures; the ones concentrating our wealth into their bank accounts.

The clutch 3 pointer is putting the worst of the lot in jail. Do you doubt their actions were intentional? Any questions about their efforts being coordinated and designed to buy the political and financial influence needed to take as much money from us as possible? Didn't they try to hide their manipulations? Are there laws on the books allowing them to steal from us? How can other countries trust us enough to do business openly when we've identified the crowd who stole from them and decided not to prosecute? Does this make us complicit? Are ANY laws enforceable that can take our pound of flesh, and give people their money back?

Our criminal justice system is about retribution, after all. Why aren't you using it? My momma told me there wasn't a better way to stop being bullied other than punching the guy right in the mouth!

What's the matter with you, B-Rock? You didn't even put your hands up…

The real game going on, Mr. President, is shifting power back to the people in this country, and not leaving our legacy, and *yours*, with the few who…what were your

Passing Obamacare

words?..."ran it into a ditch". If you don't man up, we might be hanging out again sooner than you think...

And, FYI, I'd be so totally cool with that! You Da' Man, B-Vitamin! Don't forget to send me another Christmas card, ok?

Well, enough about you. You want to catch up with me too, right? :o)

Lemme see...

Oh! Did you know I'm an insurance broker now? Yep...been one for almost 10 years and in the health care biz for about 17. I'm doing pretty well, though I've hit a rough patch lately.

Actually, that's the reason I'm writing you.

I've been reading up on ObamaCare, and I wish you had called me first before signing off on this thing. I mean, we were BOYS before you became President. You should've trusted me to get the scoop. I had your back, B-Reezy; you are President now, and I am American. It's unpatriotic for me not to pitch in, and you damn sure needed assistance.

You asked for help too, if you recall. You didn't just mean my money and my vote, did you?

I thought not! B-rizzle fo' shizzle!!!

The Patient Protection and Affordable Care Act is *awful*! I can't believe you signed off on this. I want to give you the benefit of the doubt because we are friends, but suspending disbelief can only go so far.

Do you realize you just enshrined giving over 17% of American wages to insurance companies **into law**? Why would Americans giving up so much and receiving so little in return be the best idea? The amount of money needed to take care of our health doesn't surpass 17% our lifetime incomes, so the insurance to <u>protect us from the risk</u> shouldn't be over 17% either, right? [i]

What the heck were you thinking?

Our problem with the uninsured is singular in nature, not systemic. People without insurance go to the emergency room for emergent and non-emergent care, which artificially drove up premiums for the rest of us.

This IS the main issue, right?

From my recollection, the unacceptable fact requiring change to the ENTIRE healthcare industry was the unaffordability of coverage, which increased the number of uninsured, which further drove up the price as people used services without paying for them *with insurance*, which increased the number of folks who couldn't afford protection, yada, yada, yada.

The whole vicious cycle thing...

Your solution to this <u>one</u> problem is to increase costs, increase coverage, and force enrollment by penalizing employers and employees for not getting health insurance?

You couldn't find a better answer than THAT???

Passing Obamacare

Oh, I forgot...YOU didn't craft the legislation; you let Congress figure it out. You passed the ball and told 'em to come up with something. Are you surprised they discovered boilerplate; a plan already in existence in Massachusetts...the state with the <u>highest health insurance premiums in the history of America</u>?! [ii]

B-Rabbit, you didn't shoot the rock when the game was on the line. You dished a freakin' pass...

Had you taken your best shot, maybe you could've kept the promises you made to us. Like the ones where you said "no individual mandate".[iii]

Hey! ...What about the ones where you'd go after the insurance carriers for overcharging us, or march hand in hand with unions?[iv]

Promises...promises!

Are caps on what an insurance company may charge present in the health reform law, and I missed 'em? Are things in there which will reduce costs from what we are paying NOW? Does anything in ObamaCare break up the monopolies and duopolies health insurers have in EVERY STATE IN THE U.S., providing the much needed competition that has proven to bring prices down in every other industry? Did I miss those parts when I read the law? I mean, 2409 pages is a lot to unravel...

Is nothing included along these lines?

Well????

Glenn Troy Morton

Listen, Mr. President: I've gotta go. Sorry to end here, but someone's at my door, and the banging is getting louder. I think the sheriff is trying to foreclose on our home again. I read an article the other day about squatting in your home. Apparently, the bank can't take the house if they lied in their documents, so I'm not overly worried about being kicked out. My wife and kids are more nervous than I am.

Just wish I could find a better job…

Be Easy, B-ruddah!

Glenn Morton A.K.A. Khaled Said

P.S. Oh…I forgot! I wrote this book so you can clean up this pile of donkey-doo . Please read everything, OK? You PROMISED you'd listen if someone had better ideas.

Promises…Promises :o)

P.P.S. I got next on the new b-ball court I heard you built in the White House, and I'm definitely clownin' you if your face is on half court.

Being President is cool and everything, but you ain't all that!

Preface

Why this book was written

In informational times such as these, the voices of everyday people will become the primary ones heard on human existence due to the increasing adaptation of the internet to every aspect of humanity.

In other words, the rich and powerful won't be the main way we learn stuff; we will control content.

Until that time comes, it is incumbent upon those of us who KNOW how to overcome challenges in our society to share information with the rest of us, as this will not be an easy transformation.

Power does not cede ground lightly, but will cede it nevertheless.

Hopefully!

This book was created with the idea that its existence will inspire others to share knowledge, creating a reliable way for us to educate ourselves. Recent history teaches that, in addition to trusting the sources of information largely out of our control, we should respect our own sources, voices, and expertise. There may come a day when the knowledge contained in this book, and others similar, might save you money, time, or even your life.

Hopefully…

The Internet proves we possess a wealth of intelligence among us and between us, clearly demonstrating that humans exist who, though they aren't wealthy and visible enough to speak on television or write for the media, grasp the best ways for you to protect cash, recognize a scam before becoming victimized, offer simple and effective treatments for illnesses, provide better methods of exercising legal rights, and more!

It can go and on and on and on!

In every industry, there are people making decisions and people carrying them out. Doing always brings forth more useful knowledge than deciding. It not only allows choices to be measured, but provides fuel for generating more decisions.

This idea is for the doers. You know who you are, and we need you to compete with the paid prognosticators and opinionators who might offer something better had they performed the tasks before sharing their expertise. If they built the car, took care of the patient, fired the weapon, or sold insurance, we wouldn't need to be our own reference material. More often than not, they don't. They <u>do</u> get paid to talk about it, and to advance their opinion or the opinions of their employers.

Passing Obamacare

You've encountered doers in customer service departments. Have you ever spoken to service representatives for a serious issue and they kicked the problems butt in less than 5 minutes? Well, they likely understand more and get more stuff done than everybody else around them. What about the really good financial planner who recognizes why companies do the things they do, and can help you avoid the next economic meltdown...which you realize is coming again, right?

Imagine if some honest mortgage broker, who witnessed **exactly** how people were being defrauded a few years ago, had a way to warn us. If he or she made more money writing an easy-to-understand guide, instead of participating in and profiting from our financial destruction, many of us would have been saved from toxic mortgages and the impact on our families of poorly informed housing decisions.

Imagine if we had a trusted method to help defeat the unsavory things corporations do to get money from us, and governments do to take money from us. Would you pray the knowledge reached you and your family?

If you know a reason why a certain law should pass (or not) relating to your line of work, and you feel *in your gut* that, if we understood what you do, things might be a lot better, would you want a way to help the rest of us? If you shared, you may improve the lives of thousands; hundreds of thousands, potentially even everyone.

Remember...we only get taken advantage of with our consent.

Every dollar you earn is split amongst different groups of people for maintaining the way you live as an individual and we live as a society. The federal government takes their share, as does the state, the county, the city/municipality, and the corporation.

Lack of money also reduces the ways we could live, or would prefer to live...

These numerous entities are more powerful than you and I; they thrive by having control of the flow of information and by maintaining a significant stake in your dollar.

It is necessary for you to exert yourself.

If we found a way to navigate the unfamiliar, or things too complicated to understand, the knowledge should bring us closer to keeping more of our earnings and living preferable lives, not merely acceptable existences.

Anyone interested in sharing their expertise with the rest of us must adhere to a few ground rules:

- You MUST be honest.
- You MUST be able to back up/verify what you say with facts.
- You MUST attempt to make whatever you write easy to understand
- You MUST give a bio of relevant experiences, and share motivations for contributing

If you do not have enough material to create an entire book, don't worry! I endeavor to release information to the public, so I purchased a domain called

Passing Obamacare

www.TheInverse.com . I like the name because, in mathematics, "inverse" means "containing two variables such that an increase in one results in a decrease in the other", and this is totally what I'm trying to do!

Plus, "inverse" sounds like a combination of "Internet" and "universe"…cool!

I plan for TheInverse to have the capability of gathering whatever information you wish to provide, and make submissions easy to find when you need to learn something.

I also envision creating a way to vigorously debate the submitted content and other relevant news topics as well…so bring your "A" game!

What I will NOT do is leave people to their own devices any longer. We already see the impact on everyone when the sources of information and profit are the same, and better decisions by the individual means better behavior from the collective.

I've already started The Inverse as a blog. Now, if I could just find someone to help me build it as a website…

We all hold greatness within us. The book in your hands, or on your screen, was inspired by 2 thoughts: to stop a law requiring so much from us and our children, and to issue a call to all who are truly knowledgeable in their industries, and in their particular jobs, and get them to teach us what we need to learn!

I've written what I know.

Glenn Troy Morton

Tag…You're it!

So help us and help yourselves…get writing!

Oh…and tell a friend!

Even better, share this book with the bank teller who just helped you out of a jam…she might have the combination to the safe :o)

Passing Obamacare

Introduction

In a quiet moment, alone with my foreboding, I wrote an entry into a blog that I never published, because it was meant for me. Sometimes, when I write, the words come through me, not from me...

When I ran across it again (just before I was going to publish this book), I had a thought to put it here:

"I know nothing. I have many opinions, of course. I am just not clear on what God wants from me, nor on whether or not there is a God, or even a source from which all things spring forth. When I decided to start a blog, I was going to write about being a Dad, and how challenging and rewarding it is to raise a baby girl. Then, Obamacare passed. At first, I thought it might be OK. But it isn't, so I was going to write about how hard it is being an insurance broker instead. Then I was going to write about having hope in the face of insurmountable odds. Then I was going to write about how some odds are insurmountable for a reason and how, sometimes, you need to cut your losses and live your life. Then, I was going to write about...Oh, who gives a shit about what I have to say, right? I mean, that's been my issue all along: No one gives a shit about what I have to say. Not Democrats, whom I voted for, placing the knife firmly against my back; polished tip dipped in ink to draw the PPACA tattoo

across my weakening shoulders. Not the Republicans, who can't put two sentences together about Obama without one of them being some version of Fuck You! Not the Tea Party, who could be a full third party, but never misses an opportunity to find fault with everybody else instead of creating something great. Health insurers don't like me, and are cutting me out now that they will have permanent monopolies and won't need my help getting customers anymore. My clients and employees give a shit, but I won't be able to help them soon. I am where I am...

Have you ever wanted to cash in your chips and just stop playing the game? Not in a suicide way, but in a killing your existing life kind of way? Just drive down a different road and never look back? Maybe move to a country where the dollar stretches from coast to coast, the sun always rises in the morning, and you can build a life that doesn't bring along your troubles? A place where you can begin anew...

You know why I don't? Attachments. I love my children, and their lives would be worse without me. I love my wife...and I know she would not be OK if I left, much less better. She loves me more than I deserve, and it shines through every time she tells me to pick up after myself...every time she laughs at my jokes. I love my job, and my clients are much better off for my skepticism and inquisition.

Maybe I'll be OK. Actually, I'm more sure I'll be OK than I should be.

There are people in my life that will always be in my corner, in any way that I need, and they are my family. No one else. Maybe, if they knew me better, they wouldn't be. I mean, there is ample evidence that my corner is not exactly teeming with volunteers. But they love me because of who I am, which is how I

Passing Obamacare

love them. Everyone else loves me for what I can do for them. Not just for me.

So, are odds really insurmountable? Can you really turn the tide? Can I really turn the tide? Well, if you're reading this, then you are about to find out, because my back is against the wall in almost every area of my life, and I need a way through, or a way out. I will tell you, though, that I'm not exactly optimistic, considering my track record since this law passed. But if I don't believe in me, who will? I have but one life on this earth, and then I'll die just like everyone else. It's time I live for more than just me, and put some checks in bigger boxes for once.

We need to win this healthcare fight. We need a change…"

…so I did. I changed, and I am honored to contribute the first edition of what I pray will be many contributions to come. As you've read, federally mandated health insurance is now law. Your opinion of it would be enhanced if you understood insurance the way I do.

Thank you for being open to change, and for learning :o)

Chapter One

Wake up call

I had a dream today, and it woke me up from a much needed sleep. I dreamt people were not eating, driving, hiring, enjoying experiences with their children, or doing something more important than paying health insurance premiums.

You know who you are, and so do I.

I've been in the insurance business longer than some of us live, and seen first-hand why many of you pay so much and receive so little in return. Likely, it's because you think there is no choice; forces beyond your control are causing premiums to rise.

Possibly true, although the force at issue where insurance is concerned is not outside of us, but within us, and it's a bear: a furious energy which is simply the single most powerful impulse in many of our lives. It is this relentless demon that, when it comes to insurance, I will attempt to slay for you in this book.

I'm talking about fear. What motivates insurance purchases more than fear? Fear of losing health, teeth, money, or your life. Fear of the unknown…

If you think about it, the companies providing insurance *understand this*, and try to gain business by using fear against you.

Listen to how they advertise for your hard-earned dollar:

"You're in good hands…"

"…on your side"

"Like a good neighbor…"

"Gets you back where you belong"

"Go Ahead. You can rely on us"

"Together, we're stronger"

"We keep our promises to you"

"Take away the risk and you can do anything"

"Feel better"

"Give your child an advantage for life"

These are actual insurance marketing slogans.[v] I omitted company names so as not to provide free advertising here, and because some of you are likely to rise in defense of your favorite insurer, almost as if by instinct.

Do you see a pattern? By inserting a few words in between most of these slogans, you might never be afraid again!

Passing Obamacare

Let's try:

"You're in good hands, because I'm on your side. Like a good neighbor, I'll help get you back where you belong. Go ahead! You can rely on us. Together, we're stronger. We will keep our promises to you. If you take away the risk, you can do anything! You'll feel better, and you can give your child an advantage for life…"

Well, how do you feel? Secure, like a soft, warm blankie wrapped snugly around you on a cold winter's night?

Safer, like a tightly fit condom?

Who wouldn't want this, right? Were you aware that buying insurance meant you will always have a companion who restores life, keeps promises, takes away worries, helps you do anything, and gives children an advantage for life???

If insurance were a woman, I'd marry her in a minute…

Seriously, though: If someone told you this, *and you believed them*, how much cash would you hand over to them? Do you think they send you the message, over and over, at significant cost in advertising, with the idea you *won't* believe them and give them money?

Well, here are a few numbers to chew on:

Number of States in 2009 where families averaged paying over $1000/mo. in health insurance premiums: 41![vi]

Average yearly US family premium in 2009: $13,027!![vii]

Health Insurance premiums as a percentage of median household income in 2008: **17.2%!!!**[viii]

Let that sink in for a minute. I'll wait...

Now, I expect several of you might think "Well, I don't pay $13,000. My employer picks up a portion of the premium, so I hand over a much smaller amount". To this statement, I would only say "True, but where do you think your employer is getting the money?" Insurance premiums are part of a company's "per employee" costs, and are as tax deductible as a paycheck. Employers factor the cost into overall compensation and pay their portion with YOUR money!

Don't believe me? Do you recall the last time you got a raise, cost of living increase, or a bonus? Been awhile, right? Not so long ago, some of those things were expected. Back when you had to be connected to a wall to have a phone conversation, people got at least a 2-3% raise every year to keep pace with inflation, and even _more_ if they were above average employees.

Where did the money go?

According to the US Census Bureau, the median personal income for a full time worker in the United States, as of 2009, is $47,127 for a man and $36,278 for a woman.[ix] By factoring in a 2% annual raise, the salaries would increase $942 and $725, respectively. Had you lived in New York with a family, your health insurance premium in 2008 was $12,824 on average. In 2009, the rate was $13,757.[x]

The difference? $933, which doesn't even include the higher costs you likely incurred because, to hit the $13,757 figure, many employers increased the amount employees had to pay to see a doctor or get a pill. Inflation should also be factored in, which means your dollar pays for less and less every year, by about 2-3%

Where did the money go, indeed!

I left one insurance advertising slogan out of the list. The phrase is so appalling; I thought it was worth special mention:

"...we're not in it for the money."

Do you know what makes the statement so laughable? Aside from the advertiser being a health insurer and obviously making a profit, health insurance *exists* to control the flow of money between supply and demand! What else does it do?

Health insurance companies are, in function and structure, no different than credit card companies.

I'll expand on some of the similarities within the two industries in a subsequent chapter, but please note this statement. Many people treat credit cards much differently than insurance cards. They shouldn't, but they do. The fear of being sick or dying is greater than the fear of bankruptcy…for most of us, anyway :o)

There's the word again: Fear. Fear of losing something as valuable as health is understandable. This book is in your hands because fear alone is not a good enough reason to sacrifice the other stuff in life contributing to the quality of it, and positively impacting the quality of your health. Things like financial stability, vacations, housing, education, or just plain old good times!

Did you realize stress is a major contributing factor to coronary artery disease, cancer, respiratory disorders, accidental injuries, cirrhosis of the liver and suicide; the six leading causes of death in the United States? Do you think this might impact insurance premiums, which are *paid for health-related expenses*?

I'm just sayin'...

We are now paying, on average, over **17%** of our income for health insurance, and the federal government is demanding we purchase health insurance or fork over more taxes in 2014.

Something must change.

The amount we pay in premium is NOT GOING DOWN. No agency, analyst, think tank, politician, or anyone has shown we will pay less than we are paying now; they only reveal our future *increases* will be lower, and that metric can be very misleading.

Let me show you what I mean:

If you were told you could save 10% off of future insurance rate increases by adopting the suggestions in this book, and premiums were projected to rise 25% over the next 5 years, do you think you could save 10% of your cost, or 2.5%?

Passing Obamacare

The answer is neither, since you haven't read what the premium is now ;o)

Let's say the premium is $10,000 per year for the average family, just to use a big, round number. With premiums projected to rise 25% over 5 years, in year 5 they would reach $12,500.

In the same scenario, would you save 10% of $12,500, or 10% of $2500, in the fifth year?

The answer is 10% of $2500, assuming no other factors. Your actual savings in the fifth year would be $250, which is only **2%** of what you would have paid in the fifth year ($12,500).

In a real world example, the Congressional Budget Office (an agency that prices the laws congress creates) estimates the federal health reform law will reduce future health insurance premiums by 8-11% for people in the insurance exchanges, and other subsidized individuals, in 2016.

Additionally, they estimate the average family premium for employees of small companies will be $19,200 in 2016, which is **$6173** more than the 2009 average premium of $13,027, or a 47% increase. For employees of large companies, the estimate is $20,100, which is $7,073 more than 2009's average, or a 54% increase.[xi]

Which statistic have you heard about the most: the 10% savings or the 54% increase?

Based on the 2009 median salary statistics referenced earlier, American women would have to increase their salary at least 2.3% each year until 2016 to match the pace.

It's 2011 already, ladies. How ya doin'?

If you want to improve the situation, you must arm yourselves with the only thing fear is powerless against: KNOWLEDGE. I promise you will make better decisions, reduce costs for some insurances, and eliminate others altogether by learning what's written in subsequent chapters.

If you are an employer, you can save more than half of your premium contribution by adopting some of the suggestions here, and more if you try hard enough. I will be as specific and easy to understand as possible in detailing how positive, impactful results can be achieved.

I do need your attention for the next few pages, however…

Passing Obamacare

Chapter Two

Better to have bad luck than no luck at all?

A 40 year old guy named Mr. Luck, who lives in Maryland, walks into a bar and asks for a beer. It's happy hour, and the beer costs $2. He pays $2, drinks his beer, and orders 1 more at the same price.

Clear transaction, though he might not be thinking clearly afterwards…

He gets into his car and attempts to drive. On his way home, impaired from drinking too much, he crashes into a tree, causing $2000 in damage to his vehicle.

Now, he is presented with a choice: pay for the repairs himself, or ask "someone else" to do it. He pays a fixed amount each month to "someone else" so, if he damages his car, "someone else" would pay for any repairs. He also knows that, if "someone else" paid for the repairs to his car, they would pay to fix something they did not break, and would not want to do that often.

He leaves the car wrapped around the tree and walks home. On the way, his back begins to tighten. By the time he ambles through the front door, the tightening becomes a primordial scream shooting from his ass up to the top of his head. He tries to negotiate a truce with his back by lying down on the living room couch, but it keeps getting worse. Now begging for forgiveness, he pulls out all the stops: a hot bath, a massage from his wife (lovely woman, Mrs. Luck!), and a back walk from his 5 year old son.

Nothing helps, so he gets a heating pad, contorts himself into a modified fetal position, and whimpers off to sleep.

(Can you tell I've had back problems?!)

When he wakes up the next morning, he can barely get out of bed. He clearly needs a doctor.

Again, he has a choice: pay for the doctor's office visit himself, or ask "someone else" to do it. He pays a fixed amount every month to "someone else" so, if he damages his body, "someone else" would pay for the repairs. He also knows that, if "someone else" paid for the repairs to his back, they would pay to fix something they did not break, and would not want to do that often.

Mr. Luck visits the doctor, and the doctor gives him terrible news. It seems he hurt his back so badly he will need pain medication, won't be able to lift more than 40 pounds for the next month, and will be required to wear a protective brace every day during this time. If he does not follow the doctor's orders, his back can become permanently injured.

Mr. Luck's job is in construction. He cannot afford to have his back injured, nor can he miss work for a month.

Once again, he is presented with a choice: Take off without pay until his back is better, or ask "someone else" to pay him while he's laid up. He has been paying a fixed amount every month to "someone else" so, if he could not work, "someone else" would pay him a portion of his salary. He also knows that, if "someone else" paid his salary while he was out of work, they would pay for something they did not cause, and would not want to do that often.

In case it isn't apparent, "someone else" is insurance. At first glance, insurance seems like a product that protects us from ourselves. Protects us from our mistakes…protects us from our deteriorating bodies…protects our income…protects our families when we die…protects our way of life. What you didn't see are the details in the example.

Let's look under the hood:

Mr. Luck did $2000 worth of damage to his vehicle, but carries auto insurance. His premium is the average for a driver in Maryland, which is $2134 a year, or $178 per month.[xii]

If he chooses to pay for the damages himself, he will lose $2000, so he requests his auto insurance company pay for the repairs instead. They do, less the portion he is required to contribute by contract, which is $500 (otherwise known as a deductible). His insurance pays $1500.

Since they had to pay money and did not want to, they look at the situation and determine Mr. Luck is reckless and might damage his car again, meaning more payments in the future. In anticipation of having another payment, and to ensure they will have *more money for themselves*, the amount he will pay is increased. His premium rises 20%, and is now $213 per month. ($35 in additional payment plus his existing $178 monthly bill).

They also let other auto insurance companies know they paid for his repairs, guaranteeing the competition will charge him more based on the increased likelihood he will generate a future cost. The effect of the notification keeps him as a paying customer, and secures the additional 20%.

His auto insurer will never reduce his payment unless he asks, and only after 3 years of perfect driving. Total additional cost to him: $1224 in added premium over 3 years PLUS the $500 he originally contributed in deductible, or $1724.

Total the auto insurance company paid? $2000 minus $1724, or $276.

Mr. Luck also went to the doctor. The office visit, for someone with insurance, is $150. The brace is an additional $150, and the pain medication is $50. Rather than pay the costs himself, he chooses to let the health insurance company pay for the visit. His health insurance plan requires him to contribute $20 for the visit, nothing for the brace, and $15 for the medication, or $35 total. They cover the remaining $315. His family did not generate additional medical claims during the plan year.

Mr. Luck's insurance did not want to pony up the money, and made payments like this for some of the people they insure who work in the same state, and for a company about the same size, as his.

They analyze the situation (as they do every year) and determine that, in order to keep up with the requests he and people like him will make, and have *more money for themselves*, they are going to increase the amount Mr. Luck will pay. He is married with a son, and was paying $12,541 a year for family coverage, or $1045 per month. After the health insurance increase, he is now paying $13,833 a year, or $1153 per month, an increase to him of $108/mo.[xiii]

Mr. Luck also used disability insurance since he could not work. As a construction worker, his salary was $50,000 per year, or $4166 per month. The disability insurance covers 60% of his salary while he is not able to work; they cut him a check for $2500, and he returns to work in a month.

Mr. Luck's disability insurance did not want to pay the money, and had to make payments like this for some of the construction workers they cover in his state. They analyze the situation (as they do every year) and determine that, to keep up with the requests he and other construction workers like him will make, and have *more money for themselves*, they are going to increase the amount Mr. Luck will pay.

They raise his monthly premium 20%, or $7.00 per month. He will never pay a lower amount, and must work until retirement, or age 65.

Mr. Luck's payments:

	Before	After	Difference
Car:	$178	$213	$35
How long:	*3 years*		
Total costs:	$35/mo. x 36 months = **$1260**		
Healthcare:	$12541	$13833	$1292
How long?	*1 year*		
Total costs?	**$1292**		
Disability:	$35	$42.00	$7.00
How long?	*To age 65, or 25 years*		
Total Costs?	**$84 per year**		

Insurance Payments:
Car: $1500
Healthcare: $315
Disability? $2500

Total Insurance paid: **$4315** one time
Total Mr. Luck Paid: **$5388** for 3 years min.*
*does not consider future rate increases

Yearly premium paid by Mr. Luck for INSURANCE:

	Before	after
Car:	$2,136	$2,556
Healthcare:	$12,541	$13,833
Disability:	$420	$504
Total:	**$15,097**	**$16,893**

Difference? **$1,796 per year**
Mr. Luck's salary? **$50,000 per year**

Passing Obamacare

Mr. Luck carries 3 insurances in this example: auto, health, and disability. Even though his auto insurance and disability insurance increased 20%, and his health insurance only 10.9% (how you get from $12,541 to $13833), the amount (in dollars) he had to pay was much more for the health insurance than it was for the car and disability insurance, as the starting point for his health insurance was higher. His auto insurance was $2134/year, and his disability was $420/year.

Health insurance? $12,541/year.

Not only will Mr. Luck pay out more than he will receive in insurance company payment, but he will increase his payment for the protection by almost $1800 a year *and* get no additional benefit, though he is paying more money. Does this sound familiar? Many of us find ourselves in Mr. Luck's situation.

Does it benefit him to have these insurances? Why is his health insurance so much more than his auto or disability insurance?

Chapter 3

Out of many, one.

Several lifetimes ago, a group of people came up with the idea of pooling their money to increase their purchasing and bargaining power. These "pools" of money were designed to, among other things, allow individuals in the lower economic classes more freedom, as they didn't have to brace themselves for high cost purchases, or unexpected ones.

One of the "other things", of course, was to create additional profit. I'll bet you already suspected that...

Once these pools became available to the masses, more citizens lived the lifestyle of the upwardly mobile without shouldering the burden the affluent in society were prepared to shoulder. Common workers could afford transportation, housing, and better medical care. As the size of the pools increased, many sent their children to college, improved their work environment, and became potent politically, creating a wealthier and more responsible society than could have ever existed without them.

The concept of pooling money grew to take on several forms, from credit issuers to investment vehicles to labor unions to…insurance companies. At their core, however, pooling offered a way for people to improve their current circumstances using the power of collectivism and the resources of tomorrow, for a fee.

As with all good things, the restrictions of this concept started to come to fruition. The pools grew to be so large they became influential in their own right, surpassing the ability of the individuals paying into them to control them. A dependent relationship developed between an individual and the pool to such a degree that the individual was compelled, and in some cases required, to contribute whether or not a need existed. When participation became demanded, rather than just suggested, freedoms and choices were limited.

Closer examination of the most important pools suggests this might not be the best idea.

Unions

Unions (the labor pool of money) started off as a way for workers to ensure they received a fair share of cash generated from their production, which was an important factor in the rise of a middle class. In exchange for the power to improve working conditions and demand payment from employers, unions took a portion of the workers wage.

As unions grew in negotiating power and financial strength, they became magnetic to people attracted to power and money.

This element of society eventually sectioned off entire portions of the job market and made them available exclusively to workers who paid into the unions. Non-compliance with union bosses led to violence, which helped to create non-competitive job markets. Companies offering union jobs became less competitive themselves, as the union not only controlled employer access to the labor force, but also required employers to pay workers more money, increasing the profitability and influence of the pool. The financial windfall allowed unions to extend their reach into many elements of society, especially politics and government.

In addition to their original mandate of being in service to the worker, unions became self-interested and more powerful than the workers they represented and, in notable cases, the employers creating the jobs. There is strong debate within our society as to whether or not this is a positive development overall, but no disputing this fact: the more companies have to pay to produce goods, including labor costs, the more they must charge to sell them.

When non-union competitors, from America and overseas, began to increase in number, unionized companies struggled to compete as the control unions had over the job market became difficult to overcome, for workers and their employers.

The resulting reduction in the number of available jobs and higher pricing of goods and services union-dominated companies provide contributed greatly to the demise of several industries and many corporations. You can witness the effects in places like Youngstown, Detroit, and other industrialized cities grown and nurtured with union work and union money. Once thriving municipalities became areas overflowing with empty buildings and lost dreams as corporations looked for employees not attached to the "labor pool of money". Unfortunately, some found labor in other countries.

Today, unions represent 11.9% of the US work force. 36.2% of Public sector employees (who do not face competition), like teachers, firemen, and policemen, belong to a union; 6.9% of private sector employees are members of a union. [xiv]

At their height, unions represented 29.3% of all workers in America. [xv]

Credit

The credit pools of money (credit cards) were initially created as a way for companies to allow their well-known customers to make purchases without full payment at the point of purchase, with an agreement the balance would be settled at the end of each month, and a fee charged for the privilege. Most companies kept the cards on file in the store, and sent out a bill.

Soon, the idea emerged to base the credit card on the individual and not the shop, so one card could be used at multiple businesses. The bill was still required to be paid in full at the end of the month, and the credit card company received a fee for paying now what customers didn't have to pay for until later.[xvi]

In short orders, the elements of society attracted to money (banks) realized the financial windfall they would reap by charging for the ability to pay later for purchases made now, and issued credit cards…unsolicited! They mailed out over 100 million working credit cards to Americans who didn't ask for them, creating a permanent credit dependency in our society. The mailings began around 1966, and the law stopped them in 1970.[xvii]

This time period also happened to coincide with the most carefree, anti-establishment, drug fueled, counter-culture era in modern times.

I'm sure they are not related…lol!

Credit cards became so prevalent that, instead of remaining a way for people to afford purchases they could not pay for at the time of purchase, they morphed into an entity necessary for even basic living and an important measurement for determining the trustworthiness of an individual. We have to demonstrate faithful, timely payment into the credit pool to work in many professions, several of which are not connected to credit.

As credit permeated society, it evolved into a major influence in daily life. Most people wouldn't even consider a person marriage-worthy if they had bad or non-existent credit. It became necessary to demonstrate contribution to the credit pool for making common purchases, like renting an apartment or a car. Individuals must pledge allegiance to the credit pool to facilitate many activities, such as communicating with another person over the telephone.

The credit pool also charges the business owner a fee to gain access for processing purchases, raising prices for everyone, including the ones who do not have access to credit. This creates an even greater need for people to have credit and pay into the pool.

Credit cards today are poised to replace money as our dominant method of exchange. We've all seen folks using credit to buy coffee at Starbucks, or a Slurpee from 7-11, haven't we?

Especially if we looked in the mirror…

The United States and other nations dominated by credit have the lowest savings rates in the world, and America's current personal savings rate is the lowest since 1952.[xviii]

401K's

The lack of savings, and potential for greater profit, motivated the US government to amend the tax code in 1978, creating another collective money pool allowing individuals to invest in the overall economy. Called 401K's, they were designed to be vehicles for employees and employers to contribute to individual retirements tax free. The law went into effect January 1st, 1980 and, by 1984, over 17,000 companies were offering 401K's.[xix] The plans replaced many traditional retirement vehicles and pensions offered by private industries and unions.

They also had the effect of concentrating society's earnings and giving control of our future financial capability to individuals who were tasked with growing the profitability of the pools. People who took on the responsibility were, above all, interested in the accumulation of wealth, as a history of successful wealth accumulation was a condition of employment.

You certainly wouldn't want your local barber doing it!

The enormous amount of assets flying into these funds inflated the value of stocks to such a degree that managing the money, and the people responsible for controlling it, became difficult, and volatility ensued.

Since 401K's were established, there have been several major instances of market loss:

1980-1982 recessions...the Dow Jones Industrial Average (the chief measure of economic wealth and 401K fund performance in America) fell from a high of 1,004 to a low of 776.92, a 22.6% decline[xx]

1987 stock market crash...Black Monday, where the Dow dropped from 2,246.73 to 1738.74 (22.6%) in ONE DAY, [xxi] which led to...

1989 Savings and Loan crisis...more than one-half of American savings and loan companies collapsed, the Federal Savings and Loan Insurance Corporation (FSLIC, a government agency that was responsible for insuring the savings and loan companies) was disbanded, and taxpayers paid out $124 billion dollars to save the banking system.[xxii]

1990-1991 recession...the Dow descended from 2911.63 to 2381.99 (18%) in three months[xxiii]

2001 recession...the Dow fell from 11,722.98 to 7286.27 (37.8%)[xxiv]

2008-2009 recession, where the Dow collapsed from a high of 14,164.43 to a low of 6594.44 (53%)[xxv]

Many of these wealth reductions were caused by either the people responsible for managing the money, or the ones tasked by our government to ensure that greed didn't overcome law or common sense.

None were a naturally occurring phenomenon.

Chapter 4

One of these things is not like the other…

The Insurance pool of money also had roots in a good idea; one starting in 1750 B.C. with the Code of Hammurabi. In Babylonian society, sailing merchants secured loans to finance the shipment of goods, and paid an extra fee to insure the loan if the shipments were stolen.[xxvi]

This idea can be reduced into a basic concept that has stood the test of time: if a significant number of people contribute to a pool of money used for specific, unforeseen situations, they will be protected from those occurrences, as the particular event is not expected to happen to all of them simultaneously.

To turn this concept into a business model, you must first start with identifying what is being covered and the chance of the event happening you are seeking to insure.

For example, if 100 people asked to be financially protected from the possibility of their underwear catching on fire, an insurance company determines the value of the garment and the likelihood of the item igniting. It is unlikely all 100 pairs of underwear would flare up at the same time. One might occasionally encounter a charred scrotum or singed labia…or two! However, the risk of the mishap occurring tends to be fairly low, unless someone's in a bar drinking tiger blood with Charlie Sheen during happy hour. There are exceptions to everything…

If a part of the world exists where fire-walking rituals were customary and a habit of not shaving pubic regions prevalent, then the possibility someone's panties might ignite in that location increases. In a northern climate, where frostbite is more common, the chances of boxer blaze reduce.

After determining the odds of underwear fire, insurance companies assess the potential cost. Are they paying to totally replace the tightey-whiteys for any inferno? What about the genitalia being housed in the garment? Would additional payment be required to treat charred reproductive organs? What are the chances burning around the pubic region would result in a total loss of sexual sensation (which is extremely likely, at least for me!), or the ability to have children?

From this, and other factors, insurers determine what amount to charge you for coverage, and how much to give themselves in profit. *They must collect more than the estimated risk in order to exist.* If they don't, they are not protecting against the risk of being in the insurance business; only their customers' exposure is being insured.

This point is particularly important in helping to assess your own risk, which most of us never do. Without knowing the extra amount you pay for someone else insuring your risk, you will always pay too much.

In the example of fire insurance for undergarments, let's say the price of coverage came out to $10 per person per month, and any way a human could set fire to their goodies was covered, except if someone with an unnaturally kinky girlfriend tried to claim money for their overheated genitalia, which is excluded (You've gotta know your ladies, fellas!). With 100 people insured, the premium would accumulate to the tune of $1000 per month, every month, until someone needed to file a claim.

Almost all insurance works this way. In exchange for many people making small payments, a few can be protected from more expensive, unforeseen, or unfortunate events, and the insurer keeps a portion of the premiums paid for the privilege of controlling the flow of money in and out.

All, that is, except for health insurance.

The numerous similarities between credit card and health insurance companies

In many respects, credit issuers and health insurers are in the same business, as both are intermediaries between supply and demand. We (demand) use credit cards (intermediary) to make purchases from other companies (supply) we don't want to pay for in full at the point of purchase. We (demand) use insurance cards (intermediary) to make purchases from health care related companies (supply) we don't want to pay for in full at the point of purchase.

Passing Obamacare

To reap profits for standing between us and our purchasing decisions, they do similar things. They assess the risk we represent (credit score vs. health/pre-existing condition), the likelihood of loss (non-payments/bankruptcies vs. claims data/high dollar claims), lifestyle factors which would impact our ability to continue paying (marital status/homeowner/debt-to-income ratio, etc. for credit cards; health status/gender/age, etc. for health insurance), and competitive data (what other companies are charging to address the same risk).

Notably, each charges an annual interest rate. In insurance, you might call this a "rate increase" or "renewal increase", but the only real difference between the two is the notification: credit card companies provide notification of the rate up front, whereas health insurance companies let you know just before the end of your contract year. In subsequent years, both entities give you legally acceptable notice of increases/changes in interest rate.

Can you now see how similar they really are? If so, the question before you is: Do you treat your insurance card the same way you do a credit card?

Most of the time, we should reserve our credit card for purchases we could not pay for at the point of purchase, and use other means of payment for smaller transactions. For example, charging a cup of coffee on a credit card, when the cash to purchase the coffee is in your wallet, doesn't make sense, right?

Nooo! OMG…are you nodding your head? Please step away from the Visa logo and put your hands up!

Why is this not a good idea? To answer the question, you must remember the purpose of credit cards. They are designed to give you the ability to pay for todays' purchases using tomorrow's money *for a fee*.

Therefore, if coffee costs $4.00, and you charged the purchase on a credit card with an annual interest rate of 10%, you could potentially pay $4.40 for the coffee, or even $50, depending on when you paid off the card.

By paying the full balance at the end of the month, you'd likely pay nothing extra for the coffee in the short term. You would, however, become accustomed to making many of your purchases through a third party that *exists to receive compensation for such transactions*, and the modification of your purchasing behavior would eventually result in the credit card company receiving more from you than the shopping was worth. Even if you think you're the most disciplined person in the world, no one is 100%, and many credit cards charge an annual fee.

Money, however, is 100%. Money doesn't charge a fee.

How do the majority of us use our health insurance cards? How do you? Do you charge your insurance card for a $10 generic drug?

You do, don't you? Don't hide in the back…

Passing Obamacare

Do you present your insurance card for a $100 office visit? How about a $30 blood test? How many purchases do you put on your insurance card?

Do you put EVERY PURCHASE QUALIFYING FOR PAYMENT on your insurance card?

If you do...if you use your insurance for every doctor's office visit, pill, and test; in essence, every single qualifying purchase, aren't you representing the highest risk to an insurance company, an entity that decides how much payment to demand from you based on risk?

The first instinct of health insurance customers is to lament how much they are paying in premiums. Their second impulse is to say "since I PAID such an enormous amount of money, they are going to pay all my claims, and had better not give me any lip!" The last tendency is to say "I'm still paying too much for my health insurance."

Have you ever looked at health insurance this way?

Why not? You don't act like this towards any other insurance, do you? You buy car insurance, yet never ask the Gecko to pay for an oil change or tune-up. Not even your car warranty covers new brakes or worn carpet. Why do new brakes not need coverage, but a physical exam, which is around the same price as a brake installation, require 100% coverage? You have homeowners insurance, but don't request they cover a new water heater, or gutters. Those things cost more than an x-ray.

You don't have insurance for a cup of coffee, yet the price is similar for many generic drugs.

Why do we buy insurance for such small purchases? Something that will charge us an increasing amount month after month, year after year, decade after decade, for a level of protection reaching down to every single purchase, even the tiniest ones?

Is it because the word "health" has caused us to believe our health insurance takes care of our health?

If you can admit this, you may now light a candle for the rest of us, because you're not the only one. Most people do, except the ones who work in the kitchen where the meal is prepared.

There are instances when the insurer has the authority to authorize surgeries and more expensive medical services, but this is still a *payment* authorization, not a *treatment* authorization.

Your health insurance company is only, and exclusively, designed to protect your money in the event you need medical assistance, and NOT to provide you with health care.

I've heard many people say "I need my insurance company so I can be treated by the doctor I like, and she is in their network". Others declare "my doctor prefers one carrier over the other, and I'm not getting insurance he doesn't like, so I'll just pay more for the one he suggests…"

Why? Can you pay to visit the physician yourself? Do you know the cost of care relative to the increase in premium?

Put another way: how much of a risk does the purchase represent to your bank account vs. how much more will you pay in monthly premium to protect yourself from the risk?

Do you get the answer to this question for every purchase you make on your insurance card, like you do for purchases you make on your credit card? How do you know the amount of protection you'll need if you cannot?

Credit card companies and health insurance companies are not exactly the same, however. Some key differences between credit and insurance cards are:

1) The supply is smaller and more defined for insurance companies than for credit cards;
2) Credit card companies accumulate fees and interest based on the degree of access between the supply and the demand (how many times/purchase amounts). Health insurance companies accumulate payments and interest whether an event occurred between the supply and the demand or not;
3) Credit card companies set a limit as to how much money they will make available based on the financial capability of the customer; health insurance companies do not.
4) Credit Card companies are limited by regulation in how much they can charge in interest; health insurance companies are not.

If health insurance sounds like a riskier proposition than credit cards…it is.

Chapter 5

ObamaCare...Do you want this?

Government and media reports state there are approximately 50 million Americans without health insurance coverage, out of 307 million total. [xxvii] This statistic is the prime reason reforming health insurance became necessary. The increasing amount of uninsured puts upward pressure on premiums as they seek care in the emergency room, or don't otherwise contribute to the same system the other 257 million Americans do. They also wait to get treatment until minor medical issues developed into major ones, requiring costlier care.

At least, this was the sales pitch.

More than any factor, the estimates of uninsured became proof the existing system doesn't work. Americans without insurance still get sick, after all...

While this is a pretty high count, the figure does not represent the number of Americans not insured *because they cannot afford coverage,* or who are going to the emergency room instead of a doctor's office or urgent care center.

For example, a certain percentage is eligible for Medicaid or other free medical insurances provided by federal and state governments. Several just don't sign up, even though it's a freebie. The ones who don't join are automatically enrolled if they go to an emergency room or free clinic, however.

Some are not citizens.

Another portion is single adults who decided not to purchase coverage but are not eligible for subsidized programs due to high income.

The final portions do not fit into the above categories. I've read more specific breakdowns in terms of percentages in each category, but didn't include them here so as to avoid creating a point of disagreement where one isn't necessary.

What can be done to address the impact the uninsured have on the availability of health insurance, and the costs of health care coverage for the rest of us? How does the Patient Protection and Affordable Care Act, known as Obamacare to some, deal with this issue?

It increases coverage, premiums, and enrollment through mandates and penalties.

In other words, ObamaCare adds more risk to health insurance policies, which inflates the cost of coverage, and boosts the number of people who enroll via mandated individual and corporate tax penalties, whether or not the required level of coverage protects a potential risk to the consumer.

To be more specific...here are the new protections decreed in the law:

Children can be covered under their parents plan until age 26

Insurance companies cannot:

1) Factor in the health of a customer in offering or pricing insurance coverage (no pre-existing condition exclusion)
2) Rescind coverage for individuals who fail to accurately disclose the risk they represent (medical questions on an application) unless insurers can find intentional fraud
3) Establish lifetime limits on essential benefits, like hospital stays
4) Establish annual limits on essential benefits
5) Require payment by the customer for preventative services or care
6) Sell a policy that does not reimburse at least 60% of the total cost (i.e. "actuarial value") of benefits mandated by Obamacare. This is called an "essential" level of coverage.

An "essential" level of coverage includes the above provisions and comprehensive coverage in the following 10 categories:

1) Ambulatory services
2) Hospitalization
3) Maternity and newborn care

Passing Obamacare

4) Mental health and substance abuse
5) Prescription drugs
6) Rehabilitative and habilitative services
7) Laboratory and diagnostic services
8) Prevention and wellness services
9) Chronic Disease management
10) Pediatric services, including oral and vision care

Do you see anything in the above list reducing costs? Have you realized you cannot <u>buy</u> what an insurance company cannot <u>sell</u>? Notice the limits on your purchasing decisions, regardless of the risk you want to protect against?

Are you in agreement with this?

From an insurer's standpoint, they are not able to assess their risk or limit the amount paid in claims per individual, and are restricted in their ability to design what products to sell. Were you the employee within the insurance carrier responsible for maintaining profitability (called an underwriter or actuary), how would you price such a product?

To protect the financial stability of your employer, would you assume the worst-case scenario and price products as high as possible under the law? Is a cost control provision in the law to stop health insurance companies from charging as much as they can get away with?

No.

To be fair, ObamaCare does require health insurers to spend 80% of the premium received on medical claims for employers under 50 employees, and 85% for those over 50. However, this is *profit* control, not *price* control.

There is a HUGE difference.

For example:

If I sold this book for $10, and had to pay $7 to manufacture the book and make it available to you, I'd pocket $3. Let's say the government came in and said "from now on, you can only earn 20% profit on the sale of each copy", and I still wanted $3 per sale, what would I do?

I'd sell it for $15.

20% of $15 is $3.

Based on this example, are you surprised the Massachusetts health reform law enacted in 2006, on which ObamaCare is modeled, has **the highest premiums for health insurance in the country**!

Coincidence??

If you refuse to buy into such a system, or the current one that just got screwed, you must "Pay the Man, Shirley!"

Here is a summary of the penalties individuals and employers are being required to hand over for non-compliance with ObamaCare:

For Individuals, the annual penalty for not having minimum essential coverage will be the **greater of** a flat dollar amount per individual **or** a percentage of the individual's taxable income. For any dependent under the age 18, the penalty is one half of the individual amount.

The flat dollar amount **per individual** is $95 in 2014; $325 in 2015 and $695 in 2016.

After 2016, the flat dollar amount **is indexed to inflation**. The flat dollar penalty is **capped at 300% of the flat dollar amount**.

For example:

A family of three (two parents and one child under 18) would have a flat dollar penalty of $1737 in 2016;

A family of four (two parents and two children over 18) would have a flat dollar penalty of $2,085 in 2016, as the 300% cap would apply.

The percentage of taxable income is an amount equal to a percentage of a household's income in excess of the tax filing threshold (phased in at 1% in 2014; 2% in 2015; 2.5% in 2016).

For example:

If someone's household income is $50,000, the percentage would be 1% of the difference between $50,000 and the tax threshold. Assuming the tax threshold is $10,000 in 2014, this person would be subject to a percentage penalty of $400.[xxviii]

For employers with more than 50 employees not offering coverage and having at least one full-time employee who receives money from ObamaCare to pay for health insurance, a fee of $2,000 per full-time employee, excluding the first 30 employees, must be paid.

Employers with more than 50 employees offering coverage but having at least one full-time employee who receives ObamaCare money will pay the lesser of $3,000 for each employee receiving the money or $2,000 for each full-time employee.

Employers over 200 employees must automatically enroll employees in coverage.

Pharmaceutical companies pay fees totaling $27 billion over 10 years

Medical device companies pay an excise tax of 2.3%, generating an additional $20 billion

Insurance companies pay yearly fees averaging $60.1 billion dollars.[xxix]

Is ANYTHING you've read leading you to believe you're going to give up less money?

WTF, right?!!!

How much more are _you_ willing to bear? Aren't you coughing up enough for health insurance already? Is there an alternative that can correct the problems ObamaCare addresses so poorly and reduces what you are paying NOW?

Why, I'm glad you asked…

Chapter 6

A solution that isn't this, doesn't do that, and won't offend anyone's morality

If you followed the health reform debate ad nauseum for the last few years, or just a tiny bit, a ton of residual junk swirling around in your mind will likely spring up when considering a solution to the current health insurance dilemma. The intense debate probably left you feeling fairly hopeless about the whole thing, and your instinct might be to assume that the more complicated something is, the more opportunity exists for problems.

In an effort to simplify the argument, let's start with identifying the problem:

"The Rent is Too Damn High!"
(Heheheh)

The real difficulty?

"Health Insurance Costs Too Damn Much!"

Believe it or not, that's pretty much it. Of course, this problem creates others, like the effects on people who can't afford protection, insurance companies who enjoy the excess cash and become greedy for more, and the supply (doctors, drug manufacturers, medical device makers, etc.) charging too much in pursuit of an extra slice of pie, just to name a few.

The core problem is still the same.

If health insurance premiums were $5 per month, and 50 million people didn't buy any, there would be no sympathy for their plight. Were you sympathetic towards the millions of poor, unfortunate souls eligible for free Medicaid who neglected to sign up?

Care to light that candle now?

A lower price reduces the need to fix the system, as everyone would assume things were working just fine. If the average family only paid $2000/yr. for coverage instead of $13,000, we'd talk about more important things like "what's going wrong with the Dallas Cowboys?", wouldn't we?

It's nice to have clarity…

Let's look at the factors which go into high costs as it relates to insurance. Why does insurance cost anything at all? In other words, what's the basis for the product?

Insurance protects against monetary risk; the higher the risk, the higher the price. A direct relationship exists between the risk covered and the price charged, because insurance has no other function.

Passing Obamacare

What risks are we asking health insurance to protect against? Where are our points of vulnerability? Are we asking health insurance to protect us from the costs of everything that can medically happen to a human being, physically and mentally?

Yes, we are!

We ask our health insurance policies to protect us from the financial impact of EVERYTHING medically possible, even though some things cannot, under any circumstances, happen to all people, and several aren't expensive to fix.

For example:

Men can't get pregnant. Those born white with European ancestry don't get Sickle Cell Anemia.

As a Black man, I cannot get Erectile Dysfunction...

Why does my 10 year old daughter's coverage include payment for mammograms? Why must my wife pay for obesity coverage (love you, honey ;o), or my 2 year old son need prostate examinations covered on his policy? Where is the risk needing protection?

Shouldn't we have a say in what risk we want to insure, if they are OUR risks? Is the cost higher because the customer doesn't decide what he/she wants to buy, so must purchase a product covering events which aren't a risk *to that person*? Can I reasonably expect, in the information age, to be able to decide I'd rather not provide maternity coverage, for my wife or my daughters?

From a financial standpoint, why do I need coverage for a $15 generic drug purchase, even if unforeseen? Can I pay for my own wellness visit, which typically cost less than a meal for 4 at Appleby's? Is it really necessary to protect me from every single transaction?

Is the act of living the real risk?

If that's true, we will soon become wards of the state, because all of our money would eventually go towards health insurance. Can the issue be addressed without making the situation worse?

Yes...and the path from here to there is relatively easy to take from a legislative standpoint. To start, we must identify why this condition exists and how we are asking insurance to pay for every medical possibility.

The circumstance exists due to the employer health insurance market being the dominant way people access health insurance, making the employer the customer, not the person whose income is being protected. An employer considers many different types of human beings, and does not have the capability of offering coverage specific to each employee's risk.

Not to say this isn't possible; just to say they do not have the ability now.

Why?

Health insurance companies, and the products they sell, fall under the jurisdiction of the states where the employer purchasing the insurance is based. In states, insurance companies are required by regulation to offer a minimum level of coverage if they want to do business there. State minimum plans dictate to insurance companies what needs to be covered and the cost sharing arrangement between the insurer and the customer.

In other words, states define the product.

Insurers can build on the base plan, in pricing and in covered risk, but must stay within the guidelines of the law. State governments cannot regulate coverage specific to each constituent, so they mandate coverage for everything that can happen to a human being in their state.

This causes health insurers to price their offerings based on the claims experience of the entire community, reducing the areas of competition as every insurer must sell the same thing. Pricing manipulations become the dominant method of increasing market share when premiums are high, due to other competitive factors being made relatively equal by state regulation.

For example:

You probably have a favorite soap. (I like Axe soap, so I hope they read this and send a royalty check ;o) When you go to the store, you buy your favorite. A factor in choosing to purchase your favorite is the price. All soaps are affordable, so you are freed from the consideration of price under most circumstances, and buy soap based on preferences.

If soap was $13,000 per year, you might not pick your favorite had other soaps kept you clean as well, or you might say "I LOVE my soap, price be damned" if you were rich enough. In either case, price became a significant factor.

If soap was $13000 per year, and your *boss* was buying soap on your behalf, you might not get clean at all unless you needed to be for work. If soap were bought for you and a $1000 per year price difference existed between your favorite and one which had you scratching for hours afterwards and left white residue on your skin thick enough to make you look like Nicole Kidman, your employer would likely save the cash.

If *state governments* defined what type of soap could be sold, only one kind would be available, it'd be all white, and it would only wash people with the highest campaign contributions, or the ones wielding the biggest stick during election time.

Insurance protecting against all circumstances is a luxury of the wealthy; the ones who don't decide between insurance and food, as it is the **priciest iteration of health insurance that could possibly exist**.

When price is the main consideration, the largest health insurers win because *the commodity being sold in insurance IS money*!

They have the highest amount of cash reserves available to employ the strategy of reducing premium to gain market share. Once they get the customers, they will keep them over 95% of the time as they use their dominant cash position to dictate access and reimbursement terms to the supply…the doctors, pharmacies, labs, etc.

Eventually, monopolies are created. Smaller corporations just don't own the cash to compete, so they merge with other companies or with the dominant carrier to survive. **Over 400 health insurance companies merged in the last 15 years, substantially reducing competition in every state.**[xxx]

Once a carrier can dominate the market, they raise prices without fear of losing business because no one can challenge them.

When a firm owns more than a 42 percent share of a single market, the U.S. Justice Department considers the market to be "highly concentrated", using the Herfindahl-Hirschman Index (HHI) to measure market concentration for purposes of antitrust enforcement. This means an insurer can raise premiums and/or reduce the variety of plans or quality of services offered to customers with impunity.[xxxi]

Currently, 40 states have ONE carrier with a higher than 42% market share. <u>No state</u> has 2 carriers who do not combine to own less than a 42% market share.[xxxii]

In Alabama, one carrier controls over 83% of the market! Premiums increased in Alabama 79% between 2000 and 2007, raising family premiums during this period from an average of $6,262 to an average of $11,216! The carrier's income increased by 148% from 2004 to 2007, rising from $28.9 million to $71.7 million, while its membership only grew by **5.5%.**[xxxiii]

Still think the uninsured are the primary driver of rate increases?

Were the health insurance marketplace more flexible, insurers could sell products based on whatever factors they believed were relevant, and compete with larger companies on many levels. A company might not carry the cash reserves to compete to sell coverage for everything, but might own enough to specialize in coverage for holistic medicine, and be the best insurer for that type of demand. A market surely exists for people who want to be treated by alternative medicine providers.

Another insurer may sell coverage only for women, adding maid service as an inducement, or free yoga classes and gym memberships. Coverage for couples might include massages to relieve stress; for families, a vacation package.

Offering paid incentives is what *credit card issuers* do to gain our business, because they have many competitors. They even give cash back for preferred behavior, and throw in discounts on other things, like gas.

If only insurers had the option…

Not to say it's impossible for them to acquire this capability; just to say they don't enjoy it now.

Why is it possible? Because insurers already know the numerical risk involved for everything medically imaginable. They know how many people suffer heart attacks and the statistical probability of an attack for every species of human, just as credit card companies know the odds of bankruptcy for every class of citizen.

Insurers are in the business of risk, after all, and it's never a gamble if you own the casino...

With this knowledge, health insurance companies can offer coverage more specific to the individual, and we'd be able to identify our own risk and purchase coverage protecting areas <u>we</u> think are vulnerable.

Only 2 things are needed to be able to purchase insurance in this way: a vehicle to purchase the coverage and the same level of transparency we require in anything else we consume, like food.

The vehicle exists already. States enforce mandates, but federal laws governing health insurance plans for individuals and for employers are on the books now, and they fall outside of state mandated requirements. They're called ERISA and HIPAA.

The Employee Retirement Income Security Act of 1974 (ERISA) is a federal law which sets minimum standards for retirement and health benefit plans in private industry. ERISA does not require any employer to establish a plan. It only requires those who establish plans must meet certain minimum standards.

The Health Insurance Portability and Accountability Act of 1996 (HIPAA) *amended* ERISA to make health care coverage more portable and secure for employees.

In other words, ERISA is the Twinkie and HIPAA is the creamy filling :o)

An employer gets the choice of purchasing state mandated coverage or coverage not in compliance with state law. Such coverage would fall under ERISA. Companies decide to offer coverage under ERISA when wanting to insure their own risk, and use a health insurance company to protect against worst-case scenarios like unexpectedly high claims or one time shock claims.

An individual can only purchase HIPAA-qualified plans when state mandated options through employment or COBRA are exhausted. HIPAA requires qualified plans to be the 2 highest premium plans based on volume an insurer offers, and pay at least 85% of covered benefits (actuarial value). These rules make HIPAA plans extremely expensive.[xxxiv]

By changing ERISA and HIPAA to encompass the type of flexibility where insurers can compete on multiple levels, while modifying the existing HIPAA mandated level of coverage to address the problem of the uninsured using the hospital for non-emergent care, we'd enjoy the freedom to purchase what we felt was necessary to protect our money and our health, the resulting competition would reduce prices, and more people could afford health insurance.

Before you equate what you just read with government run health care, let me state without reservation this is not either of those options. The idea isn't the federal government administering an insurance plan; no public option or Medicare for all. I'm not a fan of the federal government getting into the insurance business any more than it already is. We've already accepted federal and state government's role in deciding what insurance companies can sell us into law, and asked for regulation to protect us from predatory practices that would allow insurance companies to sell us something bad. That's good enough…

What I am suggesting is the federal government change existing mandates to provide access to broader, more specific, and cheaper types of coverage.

How would this look?

Chapter 7

Foundation of change

Part 1 – Establish a minimum federal plan

To start, we need to consider a minimum federal plan which would be accessible to the portion of the uninsured who cannot afford coverage and do not qualify for existing federal insurances like Medicaid and Medicare. These people are identified as being the primary cost driver for the rest of us because they go to the hospital for non-emergent care. Without addressing this issue, all other options are rendered moot.

We also need to know how much to charge, meaning you must be able to identify the risks involved. Can we generate the data necessary to figure this out?

Yes We Can! (Sorry...I couldn't resist!)

The data already exists. It's called Medicare Part A.

In general, Medicare part A covers:

- Inpatient care in hospitals (such as critical access hospitals, inpatient rehabilitation facilities, and long-term care hospitals)

- Inpatient care in a skilled nursing facility (not custodial or long term care)

- Hospice care services

- Home health care services

- Inpatient care in a Religious Nonmedical Health Care Institution[xxxv]

If the issue is the uninsured…if they are the primary reason the rest of us pay more and dedicate so much quality of life toward the possibility of sickness, then changing the current HIPAA requirement that qualified plans be the 2 most expensive to one mandating insurers offer a plan with benefits approximating Medicare part A reimburses hospitals for the costliest part of the problem and provides an alternative to existing state mandated insurances.

…if it were accessible to everyone; even people with a job.

This means purchasers of the plan should be excluded from any employer minimum participation requirements, so the boss isn't punished for having employees exercise their right to buy it.

This option could be called the "foundation" plan, as it would be a platform other coverage options can be built upon.

The foundation plan has the additional benefit of being dirt cheap, because there is no risk you could drive up the cost with unnecessary behavior…not even by one dollar.

Unlike outpatient services, you can't decide to be admitted to a hospital.

It isn't a Holiday Inn, after all...

Claims for the foundation plan would be paid only for medically necessary reasons, representing the lowest level of risk in the health insurance market.

The risk is so low that, decades after its creation, the federal government still gives Medicare part A away to people *for free* if they or a spouse had 40 or more quarters of Medicare-covered employment, even though eligible individuals represent the <u>highest risk of using inpatient services</u>. To qualify for Medicare part A, you must be either over 65 or totally and permanently disabled. There is no higher health or claims risk than that...

Without any Medicare covered employment quarters, the premium for an elderly or handicapped person is $461 per month for Medicare part A.[xxxvi]

Imagine the cost if you were a healthy 30 year old...

The feds could mandate a 2% load to cover administrative costs, mirroring the 2% the Congressional Budget Office (CBO) found is the administrative burden under the existing public Medicare plan, including parts A, B, C, and D.[xxxvii] Since insurance companies need only process inpatient claims with a part A-modeled product, and inpatient stays are the rarest type of claims submission, 2% is likely high...

But we can be a little generous :o)

Part 2 - Expand areas of competition

The federal government can allow health insurers to sell additional insurances as riders to the foundation plan for anything else they chose to insure. These riders can be based on common factors (such as emergency, mental health, or other "essential" provisions in Obamacare referenced in chapter 5) or, under the best-case scenario, be determined by demands of the consumer.

Insurance companies would surely engage the new product designs, especially the ones on the dark side of 42%, because they'll be able to more accurately assess their risk, which has the effect of increasing profitability if done well. They may even offer boutique plans at a significant markup. If an insurer can sell a plan with a 50% spread, more power to them. Paying the extra 50% might be worthwhile for some if it gave value in return.

An insurer might offer a plan to women without maternity coverage if a woman were unable or unwilling to have children, or one without abortion coverage for someone pro-life.

By increasing the areas where competition can be had, the possibility of competitive pricing grows, and our insurance premiums reduce.

Part 3 - Allow the customer to determine his/her own level of financial risk

One of the biggest fallacies in ObamaCare is the limits placed on our ability to decide how much we want covered when seeing a doctor or getting a pill. The minimum plan under ObamaCare must cover a full 60% of the total risk, incorporating every mandated benefit.

Therefore, if I had $10,000 saved in a health savings account, I could not buy a policy where I pay the first $10,000 for any medical services. (For the unfamiliar, health savings accounts were created in 2003 under President Bush to allow individuals to set aside pre-tax dollars for medical expenses as long as they were enrolled in a health insurance plan with a high deductible. The ability to accumulate funds continues forever. The money can be spent for any purpose, remaining tax free if used for qualified expenses or transferred to some other tax-deferred investments, and becoming taxable and subject to a penalty if not used for its' intended purpose, or prior to age 65 for non-qualified purchases. HSA's are the fastest growing segment of the health insurance marketplace.)

Actually, if I had *$100* set aside and wanted to buy a policy where I paid the first $100 of every covered benefit, I couldn't do that under Obamacare either. Obamacare mandates 100% coverage for some benefits.

Why not? If I have the cash, I can use my savings to reduce premium as the risk to the insurance company reduces, bringing home more of my own bacon every month. Shouldn't I be able to self-insure to *any degree that I'm capable of*, and use health insurance to protect against risks I cannot?

If not, then what is insurance for? Protection from NO RISK?

Passing Obamacare

We, as the interested party, cannot determine our risk tolerances under Obamacare, but other entities that profit from covering our risk, like health insurers and the federal government, can?

Oh yes, I neglected to mention that point: the federal government profits from Obamacare. The deficit reduction in this law is projected to be over a trillion dollars, otherwise known as profit. If your bills or expenses reduced by $10,000, would you say you profited?

Right...

Another wonderful benefit of the customer determining the level of risk he/she wants covered is the demand has a more direct relationship with the supply, to the advantage of both entities.

Generally speaking, the more humans involved in a business transaction, the more it costs. If you buy wholesale, you know this already.

In health insurance, the fact an insurer is between the supply (providers) and the demand (us) increases expenses for both parties. We already talked about the increase in our premiums and out of pocket expenses...what does this look like from the supply side?

Let's say the price for a doctor's office visit is $100 without insurance. To gain access to you as a patient, the doctor signs a contract with an insurance company, as the vast majority of us stay within our insurers' network. The insurer uses its provider contracts as a payment control mechanism, offering less than the physician charges in exchange for access to insured customers.

So the doctor doesn't get $100 every time an insured patient fills an appointment slot; instead, he/she may only get $60. If a physicians practice is built upon averaging $100 per patient, the other $40 would have to be made up somehow, right?

Unfortunately, the doctor doesn't actually pocket the entire $60. He/she must also pay someone to collect the money from the insurance company, as the contracts (i.e. payment control mechanisms) will not reimburse $60 unless followed to the letter…and they contain A LOT OF LETTERS! Provider contracts, like ours, are hundreds of pages of legalese, and opportunities abound for human error to cause claim denials.

Due to the complexity of collecting payment from the insurer, the doctor must contract with a company who can collect the money, like a medical billing company, *and* a collections agency for the denied claims. There goes another 10% minimum…

Now, only $54 is being collected…

By using companies to do medical billing and collections, the likelihood of full collection increases…to about 95%. With 3-4 different companies involved in 1 claim, the increased opportunities for screwing up means about 5% of your correctly submitted claims will not be paid, or more.

Passing Obamacare

Why? For a thousand reasons: bad information from the patient; processing errors at the physician's office or claims department; services performed which, while medically necessary, were not authorized by the insurer...even a full moon!

(I don't know why but, when I worked in customer service, we always took more calls from members during a full moon...Oww! Ow! Ow! Owwwww!)

Were you a doctor, how would you compensate for only getting $51.30 ($54 x 95%) for a $100 service?

If 10% of your patients are not part of your contract with the insurer (i.e. had no insurance or were seeking treatment from you outside of an insurer's network), you might charge them $200 for a previously $100 service.

...or $300.

You might shorten the time you spend with insured patients to no more than 15 minutes for new patients and 10 minutes for follow up patients, making up the shortfall with volume.

You might charge for as many services as possible per visit, maximizing revenue opportunities with each patient.

You might build in profit for every medical device purchased through your office, or accept an invitation to the "conference" in Aruba Pfizer was so happy to put on in exchange for teaching you about their new drug which, of course, you prescribe for your patients.

You might do them all...

How many of those things result in better care for the patient? This is the environment created by the lack of a direct transaction between supply and demand. When the intermediary (the insurance company) becomes so influential that it dictates terms to both the supply and the demand, costs rise and benefits reduce **for both sides**. If the intermediary had their ability to dictate terms reduced, both the supply and demand would reap increased profitability and service potential.

Using the earlier example, were no insurance involved, and the patient wanted to see the doctor, the patient might negotiate with the doctor to pay $60 at the time of service. The patient would pay less and the doctor would receive more, as no administrative cost is involved in collecting the money.

Direct payment also means the paying customer for the doctor becomes the patient, not the insurance company. Doctors would try harder to win our business if their practices were dependent on our money, and their attempts to secure customers would enhance service.

We might even get lab results on time…or a lollipop if we're good! Yummy! I want grape…

To reduce the insurer's exposure to the transaction between the doctor and the patient, we must assume as much of our own risk as possible by purchasing the highest deductible health insurance plans we can tolerate.

A person buying a health insurance plan with a high deductible is still a customer of the insurance company while within the deductible, and is only responsible for the insurer's rate for covered services, not what a participating doctor would charge someone with no insurance.

Even though the insurance company didn't pay anything, just being insured reduces your cost when using services, as the providers must still adhere to the terms of their contract with your insurance carrier.

The discounts can be very high...I've seen 70% in some cases.

Again using our earlier example, if the patient owns a $4000 deductible family plan, and hadn't used $4000 worth of services prior to the visit, then the patient would only be responsible for $60 of the $100 visit.

In other words, if your insurance pays $1, you pay $1, even if you have not used up your deductible.

Got that?

With a $4000 deductible plan, families would reduce their health insurance premiums, relative to a similar plan with no deductible, by around 25-35%, having more money available to pay for office visits and getting a significant discount on every service covered by the insurance policy while within the deductible window.

Protection is still available for unforeseen health problems, as all health insurance products have an <u>out of pocket maximum</u>, which is the most a customer would pay out of his/her own pocket in a year for covered services before the insurance company pays 100%. Out of pocket maximums are typically 2-3 times the deductible amount;

a family deductible of $4000 normally has an out of pocket maximum around $8000-$12000.

I know what you're thinking: this guy is a dumbass! There's no way my family can afford to pay the first $4000 of care. I can't BELIEVE he led me this far just to tell me this!

Ok. I understand. I want to show you one more thing...

We're ALREADY averaging over $13,000 per year for family coverage! A 30% reduction sets aside $3900 in cash EVERY YEAR that was going to the insurance company. In essence, using insurers' money to reduce premiums and pay expenses.

Funds would accumulate over time unless the entire deductible is exhausted *every single year*, which is a better bet the younger or healthier you are, and not a bad one if the only risk at issue is the remaining $100.

To use a personal example: I'm 40 years old. My daughter is 10 going on 11. We were on my coverage alone for 8 years. During this time, she had a small fracture on her arm, regular infections, antibiotics, and normal kid stuff done. I had a sore back, an infection, check-ups, and general man stuff.

Over a 5 year period, she and I generated about $3000 worth of claims. Had I set aside $2400 every year for deductible expenses (which is the lowest qualifying family deductible for an HSA plan), the accumulation in my HSA account would be $9,000 ($2400 times 5 years minus $3000 for claims). Even if I had a bad year in any one of those years, my risk was capped at $2400.

I'd save a pretty penny in premiums, too. Were it available, I might even buy a $9,000 deductible plan, reducing my monthly costs substantially.

I could easily pay for the I-Phone she wants for her birthday...and apps!

To understand why this works, let's examine how human behavior relates to medical deductibles:

No matter the deductible limit, 100% of people start with $0 worth of usage at the beginning of a health insurance purchase. We can all agree on this, right?

As the dollar amount in usage increases, the number of people who use that level of service decreases.

At $500, maybe only 60% of people use that much coverage in a year.

At $1000, possibly 40%...

At $10,000, perhaps 5%.

As the number of users reduces, the risk lowers to the insurer...and so does the premium!

By lowering premiums, you also reduce the impact of future rate increases, as they are percentage based. A 10% increase means $1,300 if you're paying $13,000, and only $910 if paying $9,100 ($13000 - $3900).

Of course, deductibles are never subject to a rate increase…

See what can be done by assuming some of your own risk? Under the above scenarios, you can lower premiums, future rate increases, and the cost of seeing a doctor or getting a pill. Imagine if you saved $20,000 in your HSA account and bought a plan with a $20,000 deductible! Your premiums might be so low the insurance companies would kiss your ass to do business with them.

This is the way it should be, right?

Many tools exist today that can improve your relationship with health insurance. Ones like HSA plans, which is Uncle Sam's way of letting us collect money to assume our own risk without taking a piece *and* allowing insurance companies to sell plans with a higher deductible.

Another great tool is patient advocacy services…

Part 4 - Require patient advocacy services to be integrated into any federally mandated plan

In many companies, the interface between the customer and the corporation is performed by the least skilled and lowest compensated employee. The bank teller, the customer service representative, the retail sales person, the waiter, the check-out guy at the grocery store…

It is the job of these employees to help us complete transactions with corporations in the happiest way possible. They are trained on manners (from a corporate standpoint, not kitchen table stuff), transactional tasks, and how to take a real problem to their superiors, but are never given the tools to help customers accomplish everything that is available in their interaction with the corporation.

This lack of availability when dealing with health insurance surfaces for the customer as an inability to achieve resolution on one phone call, because the customer service representative does not have the authority to make any changes except minor ones. They cannot pay a claim, authorize payment for a service, render a decision, or offer inducements to satisfy customers in bad circumstances.

Customer service representatives *can* take down the details of your issue and route information to the departments responsible for addressing concerns i.e. the ones who do stuff. Customers, however, cannot speak to the "ones who do stuff" directly, only to the customer service person. You cannot speak to the claims person paying for your care, the underwriter deciding how much to charge, or the nurse in utilization management deciding whether or not to authorize your surgery.

Of course, there are exceptions to the rule. Some people are necessarily very determined, and wiggle their way into speaking with someone who can actually do something. As a corporate structure, however, customers are funneled into the department for customers.

Because customer service jobs require the least amount of education and are one of the lowest paid positions within an insurer, the good representatives get promoted to departments that do stuff, like I did. The ones who stay get little reward for hard work and learning new skills because, no matter how good they become, there is only so much to be earned working in a job taking 100+ calls every day from patients. The function itself is not valuable to an insurer because their customers are mainly employers, not individuals.

In the doctor's office, a front desk person collects the information necessary to establish financial responsibility and preliminary medical data. A nurse gathers more medical information in a form which will allow the doctor to know what issue he/she is being asked to treat. A doctor treats the patient. A front desk person then provides any forms necessary to continue treatment, and schedules any follow up appointments. Other administrative staff manages charts, personnel, pays bills, etc.

At the pharmacy, the pharmacist and the pharmacists' assistants put pills into bottles based on the doctors' orders, and collect payments, from you or from an insurer. They also manage the business aspects of the store.

In order for us to fully realize the benefits of our insurance purchase, and to improve our health, all 3 entities (Insurers, providers, and pharmacists) must work together to diagnose, treat, and pay for our care. If they don't perform well, individually and in concert with the others, we could become sicker, go bankrupt, or die.

Unfortunately, they fall short many times. Each entity knows a lot about what they do, but little about the other two, and aren't set up to interface with them on your behalf.

Have you ever asked the customer service rep at your insurance company:

- "Who is the best doctor in your network to treat me?"
- "Can you research the best treatment options for my condition and let me know the findings, and which one is cheaper?"
- "I've tried to schedule an appointment with Doctor X, and he is booked solid. Can you help me?"
- "I've got a lot of medical visits coming up, meaning a ton of claims. Can you keep track of them for me and fix whatever is wrong?"

Have you ever asked a doctor's office:

- "My insurance company denied a claim. Can you talk to them on my behalf and get it paid?"
- "I know I'm covered by insurance, but I'm dealing with an enrollment problem with my insurer. Can you call them and correct my eligibility so I can see you?"
- "May I negotiate a lower payment for this visit?"
- "Can you help my elderly grandmother arrange transportation to your office for her visits?"

Have you ever asked a pharmacist:

- "I've met my deductible, but the insurance company is still charging me as if I didn't. Can you call them and straighten it out?"
- "My insurer says the medication the doctor prescribed me was not medically necessary. Can

you contact the insurer and weigh in on why it <u>is</u> necessary so the decision may be overturned?"
- "Can you recommend treatments for me that don't involve taking so many pills?"

Due to the lack of interoperability (the ability of one area to work with another area), the responsibility of coordinating the many moving parts of the healthcare system, and making them work when needed, falls to us. As the least educated and most unfamiliar, we are wholly incapable of bringing about proper resolution to every potential problem, especially while at our weakest moments physically and mentally.

The number one cause of bankruptcy in America is medical bills, affecting 2 million Americans annually -- counting debtors and their dependents, and including about 700,000 children. More than 75% were *insured* at the start of the bankrupting illness.[xxxviii] Even with the "pay for everything that happens to a human" coverage, we don't have the know-how or the energy to make the damn thing work when we need it the most.

Just because you buy a car doesn't mean you can fix the transmission. Heck, some of us can't even change a tire.

Patient advocacy services are designed to handle any issue that surfaces related to our medical, dental, and eye care. Many go above and beyond, but all do this at a minimum. They are staffed by nurses and other professionals, not customer service reps, so they know how to advocate on our behalf, and can gain access to areas within the insurer that we cannot.

Passing Obamacare

And, they only work for us.

In some companies, you get a nurse assigned to you directly, allowing her to build a history on you which will prove useful in the future and may even save your life.

Here is a short list of patient advocacy services I culled from a service called Health Advocate, of which I'm most familiar:

- Resolve insurance claims
- Save money on healthcare bills
- Navigate within an insurance company
- Assist with correcting billing errors
- Find the best doctors and hospitals
- Assist with a complex medical condition
- Locate and research treatments for a medical condition
- Secure second opinions
- Schedule appointments with hard-to-reach specialists
- Identify "best-in-class" medical institutions
- Help prepare members for visits with their physicians and other healthcare providers
- Help members better understand their serious or chronic conditions
- Answer questions and provide information about medical terms, tests, medications and treatments
- Assist with eldercare issues
- Obtain health information to help make informed decisions
- Help members complete qualification applications

- Identify and coordinate/arrange for wellness services
- Help research transportation[xxxix]

This is their CORE service, which I offer freely to clients. Total cost to me? I'm not going into specifics, because I get a great deal and don't want to screw it up, but I'll confirm it's extremely affordable, and immediate family members can access the service for free as well.

Surely, the purchasing power of the federal government should incorporate payment for this into any federally mandated plan. It is simply the highest level of customer service available in the industry, and the one with the greatest return on investment. You can't do better than medical professionals who handle everything related to your families' health care. Especially nurses.

With so many INSURED Americans falling into the numerous holes created by companies who profit by our lack of understanding, no effective solution is possible without this expertise being available to us. We will never know enough to get a fair deal or a just resolution, and our financial and personal health is on the line.

What's the best reason to include patient advocacy services? **They can help us transition to our new and improved Federal Health Reform Plans!**

You didn't want the government handling it…did you?

Part 5 – Mandate and specify insurance broker compensation for the new federal plans

I know...I know! I'm an insurance broker, so I'm supposed to say this. However, my experience as one produced this book, so you might consider that the 500,000 strong insurance agents and brokers in America, who have been working with, competing against, and battling insurance carriers for decades on behalf of employers and their employees, have a lot to offer, and you'd rather they be on your side than not.

Agents and brokers were health reform *before* Obamacare, occupying a necessary, and unique, role in keeping insurers honest and prices as competitive as possible.

An insurance broker's job is to explain products to customers, explain customers to insurers, and keep them both happy. If our clients are not happy, we generate competition between insurance carriers to help obtain the best coverage at the lowest cost. Our role is unique because, while the decision to hire/fire a broker rests with the client, the payment we receive for our services is dictated by insurance companies.

When health insurers dominate market share, they reduce or eliminate agent/broker compensation, hindering our ability to help consumers make smart decisions and increasing the ability to sell their most profitable products to the public...which they try to do as much, and as surely, as the sun rises in the morning.

If I had a dollar for every time an insurance company representative tried to sell me on the "new" product they wanted to push which, coincidentally, increased costs and reduced benefit to the customer, I wouldn't need to write this book :o)

Having no experience in insurance (as almost all customers don't), and no *access* to experience when making an insurance purchase, makes you easy pickings for every bad plan insurers could dream up.

You think premiums are high *NOW*? They'd be twice as high without our work...easily.

Taking from insurers the decision to compensate insurance brokers allows you to gain access to the best informed and most honest representation available, untainted by insurer efforts to manipulate recommendations with commission adjustments that threaten a brokers' ability to provide for his/her family.

You also get to determine how to cover your risk in the most effective way possible...

...and you don't get Obamacare!

So, there's the solution, coming in a little shy of 2409 pages...

It will work. Promise.

Final Chapter

The Way it is

When I look around, sitting in a coffee shop or at my desk, I lift my head from the screen occasionally. Not often, but every once in a while. I watch the people near me, going about their business.

Checking email.

Talking.

Playing.

Living.

They are completely unique and unknown to me.

Have you ever just looked at all the people? To think there are 300 million souls in America is mind-boggling; 300 million sets of eyes peering out into the world and making their way, as I am. It feels like being alone and a part of a whole at the same time.

I may bust Obama's chops a little in this book, but his view is 300 million strong every day, so I'm sure he doesn't pay any mind to one random American, especially regular folks like me.

I didn't think this while he campaigned. When he won the presidency, it seemed so *personal*. I was as if I became a full member of America for the first time. Not that I had bad vibes about being American before he won; I didn't. Being American was just...there.

It was subtle, like breathing. You breathe each second of every day, but never notice unless you try.

I hardly paid attention to my level of American-ness until the possibility of a President who looked like I did became real. Once it happened, I noticed a ton!

I noticed pride.

It made me become very protective of him, because I earned something in his election so profound, I wanted to keep it forever. I earned being absolutely American. Instead of me and my people and everyone else but us, I became US.

In my head, anyway...

His victories were mine, and his challenges unfair. He got the benefit of the doubt from me as if he were a family member. I always thought "Oh, he's just trying to do the right thing", in the same way some of you might say "Oh, that Uncle Jimmy! He's so crazy, but he means well", even though I'd never actually met him.

When I look around, I watch everyone thinking their own thoughts about everything, beholding a tapestry of ideas

Passing Obamacare

and beliefs with no discernable pattern. I try to imagine one so I can make sense of it all.

This old lady doesn't like Rap music…because she's old!

This man doesn't like fashion…because he's wearing a plaid shirt and work boots.

That kid is unfortunate…because her mother yells at her in public.

The girl in line is a slut…because she has on too much make up and is wearing a miniskirt, fishnet stockings, and high heel boots.

Every moment I develop an observation about someone using the view through my lens, I define them based on that view only, not on the actuality of their existence.

I never even see them. Not really.

Writing is an exercise in trying to do the opposite. It is an attempt to truly *see* people. Who are they? What do they want from me, and can I give it to them? What do they need from me, and can I care for them? What piques their interest, and can I get their attention? What do they feel for me, and can I love them?

I think these things because I'm passionate about what I shared with you in this book, so I want you to *buy it, read it, and share it.*

I want it to matter…

When I look around, I discover people whose idea of news changed with the surging availability of information. When information only flowed through a few channels, our identification was with the information itself. Opinions still developed from information, but facts drove the news.

Now we have a million sources, and things are different. Instead of our opinions being formed by new information, new information is being formed by our opinions.

News providers cater to someone's interpretation of what we want, what we like, what we need, and what gets our attention, not to the information itself. They are no longer big fish in a small pond, so they must compete for attention.

They must compete for money.

With multiple avenues of competition, news outlets make more of an effort to stand out because they have to sell for survival, and nothing sells like drama.

Have you noticed how many stories are now "BREAKING NEWS", "MUST SEE", or "EXCLUSIVE"? Those phrases used to mean more than "Hey you! Look over here!"

Doesn't it leave you confused? I can't remember the last time I heard a significant news story without someone trying to gin up some emotion about it. Trying to tell me what it means, and how I should feel about it.

I've lost the sense I'm being told facts; everything is somehow open to interpretation now…

Passing Obamacare

When I look around, I think confusion must be contagious, because it has infected everyone around me. We still hold strong to our opinions, but less so to our ability to make them mean anything. There is so much with which to agree or disagree that facts are now small in comparison to interpretations.

News Flash: Japan endures a tsunami! Can they handle it? Is it global warming? Why did Republicans defund foreign aid? Aren't they heartless bastards? Why are the nuclear reactors breaking down? Did the Japanese drop the ball with inspections? Doesn't Obama deserve some blame for not saying this or doing that! Did you know he's not really American?!

Is he Japanese??? He does like sushi...

What was or wasn't done by these people or those that could have stopped the ocean from gobbling up an island? Isn't someone to blame? Aren't the Japanese milking the natural disaster to get at our money?

Can they call their dead relatives from somewhere besides the inside of the UCLA library? For Pete's sake! I'm trying to study!

Someone, or several someone's, decided that what we really want to hear is noise. Any noise. Gotta keep new content out there! Gotta keep their attention!

Look! Up in the sky! It's a bird! It's a plane...

When I look around, I realize the someone's from somewhere have control of what we hear or see on such a massive scale that even the scale itself becomes something to talk about. The news informers become the news. Information presented becomes polarizing as we identify with commentators as personalities, though we don't know them. The sheer volume of information they present to us has the effect of pushing our feelings where they want them to be. It looks and smells like news, but it's more than that now. It's marketing. It's subjective, not objective. It's coercive...

Did Dan Rather and Bob Woodward ever have beef?

We lose trust in the fourth estate as they lose integrity, except in the one or two news sources whose personalities resemble our own. They are the only ones telling the truth! They are the lighthouse in the stormy sea of profit driven reporting...

We care about them more than we care about the news. Events come and go, but O'Reilly, Wolf, and Rachel are with us EVERY DAY.

When one of our favorite sources tells us our President is a socialist, and backs up the charge with some information and a few "friends" weighing in...Of Course! He's a Socialist!

When another one says our President is a Dictator, intent on conquering the world with our children so he can profit from destruction...Of Course! He's the Devil!

He's Hitler!

Then, we vote...

Passing Obamacare

Oh how I miss the days when I felt more secure about what I hear in the news! When the rock stars in the newsroom were reporters. The Ed Bradleys, Tom Brokaws, Walter Kronkites, and Mike Wallaces of the world; People who were passionate about THE NEWS, not developing a following on twitter.

Those types of journalists still exist. They just aren't loud enough to get our attention because they ply their trade in facts. Facts are boring; opinion is exciting.

No one notices the people who drive to work and make it on time every day; they notice the car accident. A helicopter flies over. There's a report on the news.

It's who we are.

It's why we are blind to what's being driven right down our throats. Too busy rubbernecking...

We don't mind being led down a path where we become apathetic; a path where we only rally around causes that generate emotion, adapting our energy to the 24 hour news cycle. Anything that doesn't put a fire in the belly passes by us without as much as a parting glance.

Events that used to matter for years now matter for only weeks or days. Look how fast the news turned from Haiti to Charlie Sheen; too bad for the Haitians...

We gave private banks 700 billion dollars of taxpayer money in 24 hours without so much as a promissory note. Don't hear a peep about it now. Not a blurb, a blog, or a tweet. Nothing...

I do hear a lot about jobs. How many jobs would the money have created? If "real" unemployment is 17%, out of 192 million adults over 18 and under 65, roughly 32 million people are out of work. If 700 billion dollars went to hire the unemployed on behalf of the American people, we could pay them an extra $21,875 each…about what we pay them now to sit and do nothing. They could learn new skills, or pay for the education that might increase the competitiveness of the American worker, or just contribute to our society. They could keep their homes…

We've done this before, during the last Great Depression.

The scary thing is: I thought President Obama was different. I thought he meant what he said in a way other presidents didn't. I thought he was a man of his word. I thought electing him meant our return to power, and government having our backs…

He may still be that guy, but it's becoming really clear to me that I don't know him at all. I can't see him through all the noise. I think his interactions with me are planned out and inauthentic. I think he uses the opaqueness of the noise to his benefit. I think they all do.

He always says the worst part of being President is being in the bubble, yet he didn't ask the people who know the most about health insurance (i.e. health insurance brokers) what is going on and what to do about it. He asked CEO's.

Not exactly a bubble breaker…

Having said that, I believe in my heart that the information I provided in this book was already debated over and decided against by our government. I was never in a meeting, and don't possess any insider information, but I find the idea that I could come up with a workable solution the entire federal government couldn't, with over a year to try, is very unlikely. Government is filled to the brim with people smarter than you and I.

What I don't know is why, given the unlimited information available to the President and to Congress, the health reform package winning the day is one which has been demonstrated to increase premiums higher than any other option, and not one addressing monopoly as the real driver of premium increases.

ANY BROKER WORTH HIS LICENSE COULD TELL HIM THIS; WE LIVE WITH THIS REALITY EVERY DAY.

We generate business by using competition between insurers to obtain the lowest rates for our customers. We directly absorb the effects of monopoly because it makes it harder for us to compete for new business and new revenue.

As I mentioned earlier, when an insurer has a monopoly on the market, they dictate more difficult commission and servicing terms to brokers. We represent a market that they OWN, and don't have a good alternative to sell to our clients when the dominant insurer behaves badly. It creates a dynamic where the less they need us, the more we need them.

President Obama already had his finger on the pulse of this issue. In September 2007, he gave an address to the American Antitrust Institute, where he said "the consequences of lax [antitrust] enforcement for consumers are clear...the number of insurers has fallen by just under 20 percent since 2000. These changes were supposed to make the industry more efficient, but instead premiums have skyrocketed."[xl]

He already knew...

That's why the passing of ObamaCare really makes me question my assumptions about President Obama. If he's not stupid, then what is he? Did he agree to force my children to devote more than a fifth of their income to a monopolized market or have money taken away from them in taxes?

Without even trying to break up the monopolies first?!

What would become of my babies? When I was a youngster, I needed every dollar I had. I didn't purchase health insurance until my early 30's. I didn't need to, and wasn't forced to. Does he really think we would let him do this without trying to protect our children's future, even if he IS the First Black President?

I used to tease my Republican friends about their devotion to President Bush. They liked him. Thought he was honest. Wanted to have a beer with him. Voted for him because he was a good ol' boy...

Dumbasses and ignoramuses, I thought...

Having said that, if George Bush tried to do the same thing to us that President Obama is doing, the left would've crucified him! He'd be a puppet, with the insurance industry pulling the strings. Blue Cross would be Halliburton or Blackwater. We'd march and everything!

But we don't because Barack's our BFF, and we gladly hand over our kids to him like he's Michael Jackson...

What if we're wrong about him? What if he's a Manchurian candidate who was placed in the presidency by rich and powerful corporations in a plot to take over America, our paychecks, *and* our children's paychecks?

I used to think this about President Bush. Halliburton, Enron, etc. all had ties to him, and that Supreme Court ruling was an inside job all the way, right?

What if it's even worse? What if Barack is an honest guy, after all? What if he wants more balance between the rich and everyone else but is being outmuscled? Does that mean our elected officials are really not the most powerful people in America?

Even the President???

Look at where our money's going! Is it flowing back to us, or still to the highest 2%?

What are we going to do about it? Are we living in a true democracy or not? The openness and lack of intimidation inherent in a democratic government makes it more susceptible to manipulation by the rich and powerful than other forms of government...if the voter is otherwise occupied.

We have the tools available to force change. Did you notice what's happening in the Middle East? What makes them more capable of demanding government bend to the will of its people than us?

Where is our pride?!!!

When I look around, I see you. Do you see me?

Do you see him and her? They and them? It is and it isn't?

Do you see our children?

Can you tell them all that we don't have to lock up 17% _and more_ of our total earnings into health insurance FOREVER, and anyone suggesting otherwise is not being honest, or is being given the wrong information?

Oh! Look!

Sarah Palin just ate dinner in Jerusalem, and thought the Israeli-Palestinian conflict was a "zoning" issue...

You Betcha!

(Oh God...did I just write that???)

Author's Biography

My career history started when I joined the US Army, firing rockets during Operation Desert Storm and earning the rank of Sergeant. I've been in the health care system, on the administrative side, for over fifteen years, beginning with the George Washington University Department of Dermatology. Initially, I helped process and log dermatopathology slides. I soon received a promotion to the front desk, where I checked patients in and out, verified insurance coverage, communicated with insurers to help collect claims payments, and reviewed medical records.

I earned another promotion a year later and moved to the customer service department of The George Washington University Health Plan, handling 80 to 90 calls a day from people covered by our insurance policies. Our department employed around thirty customer service representatives. When a call came in, we gathered information and routed details to the persons responsible for correcting any problems, or deciding there were none. Within six months, I became supervisor of the department and, for a time, was the highest-ranking employee in customer service.

The next promotion was to marketing where, as an Account Manager, I serviced businesses as small as one employee and as large as seven hundred. Eventually, I earned the opportunity to create and manage a new division, which I named the Broker/Small Group Services Unit. We had a staff of six and an initial budget of $300,000. We serviced corporations between two and fifty employees and over seven hundred insurance brokers licensed in our region. We addressed all of their needs, from credentialing, service issues, billing inquiries, renewals, and any business an agency or small employer would have with a health insurance provider.

From there, I left GWUHP and became an insurance agent for Potomac Basin Group Associates, where I sold every type of employer-sponsored benefit imaginable, from health insurance to 401K's. I was nominated for rookie of the year in my first year, and made the million dollar club every year in my first five.

I formed Taylor, Levi, and Associates LLC, an independent brokerage firm, in 2009.

In addition to my professional life, my wife is Alicia, my 2 children are Taylor and Levi, and my 2 step-children are Abby and Jakobi. We reside in Maryland.

Notes

[i] http://usgovinfo.about.com/gi/o.htm?zi=1/XJ&zTi=1&sdn=usgovinfo&cdn=newsissues&tm=8&f=20&su=p284.9.336.ip &tt=2&bt=1&bts=0&zu=http%3A//www.census.gov/prod/2002pubs/p23-210.pdf; and http://www.ncbi.nlm.nih.gov/pmc/articles/PMC1361028/; compared

[ii] http://www.ncsl.org/default.aspx?tabid=14514

[iii] http://campaigncircus.com/video_player.php?v=6130

[iv] http://www.foxnews.com/politics/2011/02/25/obamas-promised-march-union-workers-fails-materialize/

[v] http://www.textart.ru/database/slogan/insurance-advertising-slogans.html

[vi] http://www.ncsl.org/default.aspx?tabid=14514

[vii] http://www.ncsl.org/default.aspx?tabid=14514

[viii] http://www.commonwealthfund.org/~/media/Files/Publications/Data%20Brief/2009/Aug/1313_Schoen_paying_the_price_db_v3_resorted_tables.pdf page 10

[ix] http://www.census.gov/prod/2010pubs/p60-238.pdf page 11, figure 2

[x] http://www.ncsl.org/default.aspx?tabid=14514

[xi] http://www.cbo.gov/ftpdocs/107xx/doc10781/11-30-Premiums.pdf page 8, first sentence

[xii] http://www.carinsurancequotes.com/maryland-car-insurance.php

[xiii] http://www.ncsl.org/default.aspx?tabid=14514

xiv http://www.bls.gov/news.release/union2.nr0.htm Third paragraph

xv http://www.unionstats.com/ ; "State Union Density in the U.S., 1964-2010 Copyright 2011 by Barry T. Hirsch and David A. McPherson

xvi http://www.creditcards.com/credit-card-news/credit-cards-history-1264.php

xvii http://en.wikipedia.org/wiki/Credit_card; http://www.pbs.org/wgbh/pages/frontline/shows/credit/more/life.html

xviii http://www.bea.gov/national/nipaweb/Nipa-Frb.asp

xix http://www.ebri.org/pdf/publications/facts/0205fact.a.pdf;

xx http://useconomy.about.com/od/stockmarketcomponents/a/Dow_History.htm

xxi http://useconomy.about.com/od/stockmarketcomponents/a/Dow_History.htm

xxii http://useconomy.about.com/od/grossdomesticproduct/p/89_Bank_Crisis.htm

xxiii http://useconomy.about.com/od/grossdomesticproduct/p/89_Bank_Crisis.htm

xxiv http://useconomy.about.com/od/grossdomesticproduct/p/89_Bank_Crisis.htm

xxv http://useconomy.about.com/od/grossdomesticproduct/p/89_Bank_Crisis.htm

xxvi http://en.wikipedia.org/wiki/History_of_insurance

xxvii http://www.census.gov/prod/2010pubs/p60-238.pdf; page 24, figure 7

xxviii https://www.bcbsri.com/BCBSRIWeb/pdf/Individual_Mandate_Fact_Sheet.pdf

xxix+NATURE OF A SUBSTITUTE TO H.R. 4872, THE "RECONCILIATION ACT OF 2010," AS AMENDED, Fiscal Years 2010 – 2019 H.R. 3590, THE "PATIENT PROTECTION AND AFFORDABLE CARE ACT ('PPACA')," AS PASSED BY THE SENATE, AND IN COMBINATION WITH THE REVENUE EFFECTS OF SCHEDULED FOR CONSIDERATION BY THE HOUSE COMMITTEE ON RULES ON MARCH 20, 2010"; page 2

xxx http://hcfan.3cdn.net/dadd15782e627e5b75_g9m6isltl.pdf

xxxi http://www.justice.gov/atr/public/guidelines/horiz_book/15.html

xxxii http://hcfan.3cdn.net/4cca2e20e9435e76ab_r3m6bxre3.pdf

xxxiii http://hcfan.3cdn.net/cf37cd396f076327af_r0m6bx6j0.pdf

xxxiv Health Insurance Portability and Accountability Act of 1996, Title , Pub. L. No.104-191, Section 2741(c)(2) , (Aug 21, 1996).

xxxv http://www.medicare.gov/navigation/medicare-basics/medicare-benefits/part-a.aspx?AspxAutoDetectCookieSupport=1

xxxvi

https://questions.medicare.gov/app/answers/detail/a_id/2260/~/medicare-premiums-and-coinsurance-rates-for-2010

xxxvii

Congressional Budget Office, "Designing a Premium Support System for Medicare," November 2006, 12

xxxviii

http://www.consumeraffairs.com/news04/2005/bankruptcy_study.html

xxxix

http://www.healthadvocate.com/core_health_advocacy.aspx

xl Barack Obama, "Statement of Senator Barack Obama for the American Antitrust Institute," September 2007. Accessed at http://www.antitrustinstitute.org/archives/files/aai-%20Presidential%20campaign%20-%20Obama%209-07_092720071759.pdf

Made in the USA
Charleston, SC
18 May 2011